A BRIDGE TO THE GENERATIONS

Borgo Press Books by JOSEPH REBHUN

A Bridge to the Generations: A Personal Memoir Inspired by the Experiences of Marie Rebhun
Crisis of Morality and Reaction to the Holocaust
The Embers of Michael: A Historical Epic
God and Man in Two Worlds
Why Me? Memoirs of Holocaust Survivors

A BRIDGE TO THE GENERATIONS

A Personal Memoir Inspired by the Experiences of Marie Rebhun

by

Joseph Rebhun

THE BORGO PRESS

An Imprint of Wildside Press LLC

MMIX

Studies in Judaica and the Holocaust
ISSN 0884-6952

Number Four

Copyright © 2009 by Joseph Rebhun

All rights reserved.
No part of this book may be reproduced in any form
without the expressed written consent
of the author and publisher.

www.wildsidebooks.com

FIRST EDITION

CONTENTS

Prologue: To My Grandchild 7
Chapter One: Pre-World War II Warsaw 13
Chapter Two: Germany Invades Poland (1939)............27
Chapter Three: Russian Occupation................................37
Chapter Four: Attending the University of Lvov...........42
Chapter Five: Living in Lvov After Ejection from
   the University 46
Chapter Six: Vilno, Lithuania (January 1941) 52
Chapter Seven: Latvia 56
Chapter Eight: Working in Vilno 60
Chapter Nine: Germany Occupies Vilno (June 22,
   1941) 64
Chapter Ten: Escape...67
Chapter Eleven: The Ghetto...73
Chapter Twelve: Temporary Sanctuary 80
Chapter Thirteen: Work Outside the Ghetto 84
Chapter Fourteen: Moral and Physical Health 87
Chapter Fifteen: Life in the Ghetto 93
Chapter Sixteen: The German "Action" (Spring,
   1942)..98
Chapter Seventeen: From Ghetto to Camps.................111
Chapter Eighteen: Death March (October, 1944) 135
Chapter Nineteen: Liberation 141
Chapter Twenty: A New Beginning..............................148

Chapter Twenty-One: From the Abyss to the
    Summit 165
Chapter Twenty-Two: Our Home 194
Chapter Twenty-Three: My Loss 197
Chapter Twenty-Four: Alone 200

PROLOGUE

TO MY GRANDCHILD

Dear Grandchild:

On your thirteenth birthday you know how to operate computers much better than your grandfather. You are much better acquainted with the scientific achievements of the twentieth century than I was at your age, and you even understand business better than I ever did. But there is still something that you could learn from your "*sabah*" (Hebrew for grandfather): the depth of love, of loss, and of suffering. I would hope that you are touched in life exclusively by the first of these, but that the existence of the other two does not remain unfamiliar to you and also, that you walk down the path of righteousness and morality and see the world as the Creator formed it, rather than as man distorted it. You should identify yourself with a set of values, which add meaning to life and to its moral foundation.

Try to understand the greatness of the universe and the power of the energy that rules it and its constant changes and disturbances that are beyond human control. Studying physics, you learned about the duration of longitudinal waves. They can, however, be disturbed in their conveyance by a transverse wave, which may result in havoc.

Your maternal grandparents survived such a transverse wave, caused not by nature, but by human beings. They survived this destructive transverse wave by chance or by a miracle and, like two waves driving in the same direction, they reinforced each other and became one, until your grandmother was separated from us and was gone forever. This might not be easy for you to understand, but no matter how painful it was for us, it is a normal conveyance of life, as it is with other human beings, with civilizations and nations, a conveyance from one state of existence into another. Similar to this is a conveyance of cosmic forces around us with the formation of new forms and with the disappearance of the old ones. Recognition of these forces while accepting the idea of their Creator is the basis of theological revelation. We can do nothing about cosmic forces, but we can and must control the morality of man, outlined at Mount Sinai in the Ten Commandments. On the day of your maturity, you must accept the existence of the Creator and follow a moral code. Today you become a link in the chain of history and tradition of the people who accepted these spiritual ideas. The holiness of service to the Creator is demonstrated by service to His creation. Applying moral standards in your daily acts, no matter how hard it might sometimes be, with the cognizance of the world's Creator, is a requirement for you to become a member of our religious group, of the Jewish religion. The consciousness of ethical behavior imprinted in your heart will become your eternal treasure. I bless you so that you will grow in this effort to learn goodness, justice and admiration of the creation.

In order to be closer to the Creator, you have to discover yourself, as everybody else must. Your eye may have to turn to a drop of rain for an answer, instead of to man. Look around you. The uniformity of the blue sky without a speck of clouds makes you retain and eternalize the picture of tranquility. Other people and even animals seem to enjoy life, hoping that it will last forever and that it is the panorama of paradise.

But sheets of clouds sneak in during the stillness and cold of the night, close to each other, touching and kissing the neighboring clouds, diffusing in each other and becoming a darker, heavier mass, whose molecules wait for the next act of nature. Now animals don't relax and crows scream, flying rapidly over homes and trees, as if feeling the approaching storm. Only some people say that blue skies become monotonous and there is need for change, that the dry surface of the earth could use some heavenly watering. The winds start to bend the branches, blowing down the yellow leaves. There is a definite undulation of the elements. Older people saw these explosive changes of nature in the past, following calmness, and they felt uneasy, similar to the animals. When the storm finally came and left a path of devastation behind, some pretended that it was an exhilarating stimulating experience and that they were the courageous ones. The surviving green elms and the burgundy crowns of maple trees knew the real history of the people. Only some old men admitted the excess of natural forces and saw a similarity with human history. Some people have a premonition of coming dangers, but only very few try to change or evade them. After the storm passes, some minimize it, some capitalize on it and some even lie about it, saying it never occurred and enrich themselves at the cost of the survivors, who carry the memory of losses and the burden of truth.

If you want to know more, ask the transparent drop of rain remaining after the storm. It has a history of freezing, melting and vaporizing, migrating in waves of clouds that exist no more. It is only a drop, but it has lived through many perplexities. It is a small pear-shaped quantity of water, which is indispensable for life. It might have existed at the time when the Ten Commandments were given on Mount Sinai.

You would like me to tell you how to find God. This can be done only by the strain of your own spiritual eye. Send out the searchlight as strong as you can all over the universe; even if you should not get back a reflection, the search itself is uplifting It is individual, yours. It points to the oneness of creation and to the interdependence between yourself and the non-self world around you. You have to find this yourself. I experience the peaceful reward of this search daily.

Both your grandmother, if she were alive, and I, could not only tell you about God, but about the code of behavior assuring the coexistence of the self and non-self, about morality. We got our knowledge from our experience of the greatest immorality in human history. What we learned was that you will not find the appreciation of God's creation in theology, legality, education, or in technology. The psalm describes men creating gods in their own image: *K'mochem ihyou osejchem.* In the name of the falsely perceived God, more people in history were killed than saved. The laws of the country always represented people who controlled power: the laws of Nazi Germany recommended and sanctioned the killing of Jews, and Himmler attached to this action the word *morality*. Physicians, lawyers and others with a higher education in Nazi Germany committed heinous crimes. Germans at the time of Hitler were the most educated people on earth. Also, the newest explosion of technology could be reversing its intended benefits for human society, into misdeeds and possibly become detrimental for all mankind. We see that this has already happened with chemical, nuclear and bacteriological research.

What I am leaving with you today is a lesson of love of God expressed by the love of all His creation. How to embrace the world around you with love is the essence of Judaism. This should be an intense, never ending effort on your part, a process, which should bring you happiness in spite of some possible disappointments. Conditions around us change, but we must persistently follow the imperative to preserve our own life and the life of those who are dear to us without causing harm to others existence. By combating immorality you will know that you did your part and that you have chosen good over evil. There are no eternal, unchangeable forms of creation. New forces and forms replace old ones, but we are granted a certain time to make the right choice, regardless of the end results. We must ride the crest and not succumb to the forces of evil, which fortunately has only a limited time of existence on the waves of history.

Cosmic occurrences and human history show a similar undulant course, which we are reminded of by the life cycles of individuals. Common to all the changes that occur in individual people is a force we believe will persist after all else vanishes. Neither I nor anyone else could tell you much about it. It is the creating force, unknown, but felt by all the fibers of living beings. Even though nobody can describe that force to you, you could perhaps get some more information from the transparent droplet of water, which froze, melted and evaporated to eventually fall from the clouds in order to support life.

Let me now share with you the story of the life and thoughts of your grandmother, Marie, and some of the common experiences that we had together. This is as she would have told it to you.

CHAPTER ONE

PRE-WORLD WAR II WARSAW

Let me start by telling you about Warsaw, the city in which I was born, about my school, family and friends, the social scene just before the war.

Life in Warsaw, the capital of Poland, was quite different from that of the provinces. While our country was known at that time as the romantic bread basket of Europe, from whose rye fields and stables flour and butter was exported to England, the cities became the place where commerce, craft and professions started to blossom. Warsaw was a cultured city and we felt part of it, but we never felt secure, even though our Jewish ancestors lived in this country for almost a thousand years. In the big cities the competition for jobs and education was fierce, especially felt during times of global depression. I had to face these economic difficulties beginning in early childhood.

We made a mistake, as many people probably did, in that we felt we were Poles. We were in love with the country, with the cultural assets. My family has been in Poland for many generations. So we always were proud of the literature, poetry, and art and we always realized that the Jews contributed so much to those fields. We had many poets and writers of Jewish extraction. They were really the best Poles that you could find, but they seldom even wrote on the subject of the Jews.

At the time that the Russians occupied this part of Poland, before the First World War, there were restrictions against Jews. There were so-called May Laws that were established at the end of the nineteenth century, the so-called Pale of Settlement, areas in which the Jews could live. They couldn't settle out of those areas. Under Russian rule in Warsaw itself, there were great restrictions, especially in the field of education. As the twentieth century drew nearer, these restrictions had not yet been relaxed, but Jews found some loopholes.

My family on my father's side was mainly from Russia and Latvia. The same story took place in Russia as during the Second World War, during the Hitler era, when the idea of the annihilation of the Jews was conceived. There were some Jews called *Nutzliche*, which means that they were needed by the German government. They were economic assets. This applied to my family. Of course, I never realized this, but I remember that it was inherited from generation to generation. They were called *poczotnyj grazdjanin*. It meant that one was a 'noble citizen,' needed by the imperial regime, considered an asset. And they brought this into Poland when they came into Warsaw, which at that time was the Grand Duchy of Warsaw.

During the time of Poland's independence university restrictions for Jews continued. There was the quota system, *Numerus clausus*, which meant that only a certain percentage, I think three to ten percent, could attend the colleges. But some cities had so-called *Numerus nullus*. It meant that nobody of Jewish extraction could enter a college. But in Warsaw there were not similar restrictions. Jews always wanted to get an education.

When I was a child, ten years old exactly, our economic situation deteriorated very much and I stopped going to the private school of Mrs. Lange. I was very promising in school and did really well, but there was no money.

In Poland, in order to get an education in a private school, you had to pay. Grammar school was free up until the fifth grade. The fifth grade marked the starting of the Gymnasium, which would be at eleven years of age. It was like high school here.

At this time my father died at thirty-four years of age. It happened like this: my grandmother was a society woman and he accompanied her on a big tour of Europe. He was killed in an airplane crash. My mother was very young with three small children and she could barely manage. Our wealth dwindled. My mother remarried, but her new husband was somebody of much lower social status. It was maybe because she had children and couldn't cope with the situation. I felt very depressed because I missed my father. My stepfather was very good and I called him 'father.' He had three children of his own and we called each other brothers and sisters. There were his three and our three children, and then there was a child born in mother's second marriage. So our family was big.

I decided to start work when I was ten. I worked in a big salon making hats, *modiste*. After ten months I got fed up and decided this was not for me because, all day long, the workers only talked about their-the love affairs. They were the professional girls.

There were so-called public schools in Poland, but the status symbol was attending a private school. Social opinion was very important. Maybe you would be hungry, but nobody was supposed to know about it. One always had to show a different face. One always had to pretend. You would go in the street every day dressed neatly in your best Sunday clothes. According to our standards in Poland, people who shop here are shabbily dressed. A lady always went shopping with her hat and gloves. It was the same story with schools. It was just beneath your dignity among our friends to send your child to public school.

After that year of working I told my mother that I was

going back to school and that I would work. And I did. I started to make money by tutoring so that I could pay for school. I went to a private school. In that private school we paid our tuition on a monthly or half-monthly basis, depending on how much money you had. This was a non-sectarian, Polish, non-Jewish private school for girls. This was a school designed to give the girls a good upbringing and good manners—so-called *Kinderstube*. I never went to church. But there was no instruction in the Jewish religion. In the morning at school you said the Lord's Prayer and when you left you said another prayer. I liked movies and I adored Shirley Temple, but I rarely had time for that pleasure.

Friday night my brothers went always to the synagogue. We lit the candles and said the prayer. It was a very beautiful celebration. Otherwise I really did not know too much about Judaism. The boys knew. I felt strongly as a Jewish girl, but I did not understand too much about religion. But a few years later, shortly before I graduated from this school, we were given time for religious instruction and we had a teacher. The Jewish children came to this teacher from a few schools. He never taught us Bible but he taught us Jewish history, which I feel is a wonderful thing because those were things you really appreciated in life.

In addition, I had a little religious upbringing at home because we celebrated all the holidays in a beautiful way. On Saturdays, according to our religion, one rested and did not work, but on Saturday I had to attend school. Otherwise, we did not work. I remember how our family was gathered at the table covered with a white tablecloth. We were considered the more religious Jews to be tending to assimilation. I don't know if it was true because we really practiced Judaism and associated with it very much.

I went to this private school for two years where I got also my piano training. I tutored other students in math and French. It would have worked out well, but I was young and they took advantage of it and did not pay me regularly and I just collected a fraction of my salary. The people who owed me the money were rich and they were living in a very fancy area, but they were kind of mean.

There were other types of schools called government schools. They were the equivalent of our high school but with a little bit higher programs. Here you did not have to pay tuition. They were the top as far as the education they offered. It was very hard to get in, especially for a Jewish child. Maybe four or five hundred students applied, and they would only accept twenty. I passed the examination and was admitted to that school. You had to work very hard and I was in attendance there for four years until I graduated.

You had no options, no electives. You took math, physics, chemistry, literature, history, geography, and philosophy. Everybody had to take it. When you graduated you received your baccalaureate. It was a fairly well rounded education.

At that time I was qualified to apply to a college. I went to the University of Warsaw. The war broke out and I finished the four years in Lvov during the war. I studied law and finally graduated.

When I was in school the students had very good, very friendly relations and only on several occasions, when the girls forgot, they would let me know who I was. You see, I didn't even realize this. Maybe they really did not mean it.

The university was not a private one. It was supported by the state. The cost was one hundred and ten złotys. As you can see, I worked very hard all my life and, even as a young girl, I did a lot of teaching. I had older brothers. My mother decided that she really wanted to give them a good education. First, she decided that one my real brother would go to study medicine. It was almost impossible at that time for a Jewish boy to be accepted. She decided that she was going to achieve it, but nobody could believe it. My brother was successful and he was accepted. My mother was a wonderful person—very intelligent, very cultural, with great tastes and she knew about life. She was not university educated because she had married at the very early age of sixteen, but she was very educated otherwise. When she decided that her son was going to study medicine, she went to the dean of the medical school. Nobody wanted to let her in, and she had to use all possible methods. Finally, she got to him and told him that her son didn't have a father and that he was very gifted. It was an asset that he had graduated from the governmental school with honors. He really did well on the entrance examination and was accepted. It was much harder to get into medical school in Poland than in the United States. He started shortly before the war his private practice, attending the renowned Jewish hospital at the Czysta Street.

My other brother was quite sick as a child and we were glad when he graduated and went to study law. When you graduated from law school in Poland, you had to work in court as an intern. This lasted three years and you were paid just a nominal fee like the medical interns here. After completing the court internship, you had to intern at a lawyer's office for two years. Then, after successfully accomplishing the training, you had to pass the bar exams. Before that, at the end of each school year, you had to pass exams. We did not attend classes too much. This helped us because you had to work to support yourself. When you graduated, it was very difficult for Jews to get assigned to a court.

My mother was instrumental in my brother's private internship. There was a very prominent lawyer in Warsaw and he was the brother-in-law of the famous Pilsudski. His name was Ludwig Szczerbinski. He was genuinely a very nice man. My mother went to him and I don't know how she influenced the lawyer, but she was successful and he accepted my brother. This was the best-known legal office in Warsaw. My brother worked there and he got a wonderful experience being associated with this eminent lawyer. He worked there only one year.

Poland was just a powder keg before the war. Anti-Semitism was on a rampage. After the death of Marshal Pilsudski, the entire Polish society and especially the Jews became depressed, and soon thereafter, the right elements took charge of the government. Nationalism turned into chauvinism, which increased just before the war. I just speak of my own experience. The discrimination was felt almost everywhere.

To be accepted for medical studies became unattainable for the majority of Jewish students, but my mother was able to break the barriers. My stepsister wanted to study dentistry and went to medical school. To become a dentist you had to go to a medical school. And we were successful in getting her accepted.

When you were a Jewish student, conditions were fine at the beginning of basic training. Later there was discrimination. You couldn't get patients. You had to bring your own patients and the schools wanted the Jews to deliver Jewish corpses in order for them to study anatomy and pathology in the practical laboratories. According to the orthodox Jewish religion you could not do this.

The school probably knew this. You didn't have to be an orthodox Jew to adhere to the religion very much. I remember when my brother and sister came home complaining, 'What are we going to do?' They stayed at home for more than a week. I don't know how they solved this problem later, but they probably found a solution.

My stepbrother, Stas, went to study engineering. There was an excellent school in Warsaw, something like MIT. He graduated from that governmental school also. As it happened, everybody graduated shortly before the war. On one hand, the tension and the pressures were mounting.

After you graduated from school, you could establish yourself and then start thinking of building a family. You had to be established, to have some economical basis. Stas got a wonderful job with a big engineering firm. So again we were very happy because everything worked out nicely. Each child contributed some money to support the family, because by this time our family was large and there were big expenses. The firm my brother worked for had some government orders. As anti-Semitism was on the rise, my brother's employer realized that he was a Jew. One couldn't change names or assume a different one. But it so happened that my stepfather had a good Polish-sounding name, Zmijewski. When you heard this name people would very often assume that you were not a Jew. This was the case with the engineering firm. When the firm found out that Stas was Jewish, he immediately lost his job. He felt very bitter about it, more so since he had met a very sweet girl and he wanted to marry her. He went on a trip to the United States.

The year was 1939. I had not yet graduated. I was the youngest, except for Zosia, my sister, whom my mother had with her second husband.

The fascistic waves were inundating Europe from Spain eastwards incorporating Italy and Germany. They threatened to collide eventually with the Soviet dictatorship. They resurrected the old ideas of religious and ethnic prejudice, which were ingrained in the neutral countries, especially Poland. The newly born nationalistic parties were poised against the Jews. The future appeared bleak.

The Jewish community was not only affected by the political and economic atmosphere, but also by the changes within. The daring younger generation was finding its own ways and was split from the orthodoxy.

The university had its own court of law. It was autonomous. It was not under the jurisdiction of the local city police. And this was the biggest crime in my understanding. Sometimes awful things happened at the universities. I did not often attend the university, but, of course, having contact with the students, I witnessed terrible things. In 1938 and 1939 this happened more and more often. The Roman Catholic Church stepped into the political arena not officially, but by its spiritual authority, trying to restrict Jewish business and activities, and falsely accusing Jews, as the non-believers, of transgressions against Christianity. The Church was responsible for the anti-Semitism, which reached the roots of the society with small exceptions. The hatred of Jews blossomed on the spiritual soil of a very religious people.

The ultra-radical, extreme elements (we didn't even call them chauvinists but just called them 'the patriots') felt that there was no room for the Jews. They would have just liked to drown them all in the sea. So they started to fight the Jews in the universities. The students were like a para-military organization. They used to come to the colleges and bring braces or little knives. By our standards this is unheard of. The fighting took a few hours and though there was a university police force, they always happened to disappear at just that moment.

The very radical elements were very much in the majority in 1938 and 1939. They weren't all fighting, but everything was called spontaneously Suddenly they assembled. They started to spread false rumors and always found some kind of incentive. They falsely accused the Jews of animosities and hostilities. The Jews were among the best students, hard-working and friendly, willing to help and to cooperate. But they were always looked upon as the underdogs. Eventually the students, the National Democrats, were not only fighting the Jewish students but went out into the wider Jewish Community.

You see, when I went to school, I had many friends. I did not look like a typical Jew. As a matter of fact, they used to say that I was not a Jewish girl. I was light blond with blue eyes. I spoke meticulous Polish. It was very easy for me to mingle and nobody would question whether I was a Polish girl. I didn't have anything really specifically Jewish in myself. How the Poles would look at me! I didn't consider this an asset, but later, this will help you understand many things and perhaps why I really survived the war.

I heard so much about the pogroms. I always wanted to be a witness—I always happened not to be around or to come too late and so forth. In January of 1939 I was walking in the street. I was really in a very good mood and happy and I was rushing to tutor some students. Suddenly I saw something happen. Quite often something happened in the streets in Europe. People expressed their feelings and passions. I saw a few people—one or two well-dressed people, the rest badly dressed. A few men incited to riot. It started like that and spread. They said, "Let's go and get the Jews." It started just by word of mouth. Right away they went into the middle of the street. We did not have too many cars before the war, but we had carriages. So the carriages pulled to the side. They chose a special route so that no streetcars ran through. In a matter of a minute they had two hundred people and they started to look into the eyes of everybody passing on the street and tried to recognize who was Jewish, "Is he a Jew or not?" They had to do it this way because Warsaw had quite a large number of Jews (350,000), one third of the total population of the city.

There was a man passing just then, maybe a grandfather with a young grandson. They approached him, put his arms behind his back, and started to pull his beard, to laugh and to push him. The little boy started to cry, "Mercy, mercy." I felt very badly. In order to see better what they were doing, I joined and mingled with the crowd to see what would happen next. It was just terrible. You couldn't take it when you saw the misery. While the crowd was bending and beating the victim, I saw him only holding on to his hat with a stony expression on his face. He did not utter a word. This scene expressed all the religious intolerance and hatred. It went on and on. Whomever of the Jews they spotted, they pushed. I did not see that they used knives, but I imagined that there were cases where they were used.

People were pushed to the ground, kicked, and knocked in the teeth. You couldn't watch it. My eyes were full of tears and the Poles couldn't understand why I cried, because they thought that I was one of them. This went on for maybe five hours. And somehow, nobody saw this, despite the fact that we had a very good and efficient police force in town. And the laughter, the joy, accompanied the beating.

Finally the Jewish proletariat, the working class and particularly butchers in Warsaw, decided to fight back. They organized a resistance group, and when the attackers came, they started to hit them back. This was the only way they counteracted. Only self-defense finally brought order because the police did nothing. Once strength was met with strength, order was seen. Interestingly enough, I want to say that this was the Jewish proletariat, not the Jewish intelligentsia or students or other members of the Jewish population. Just the working class was fighting. It is important, because later, in the Warsaw Ghetto uprising of 1943, it was the young proletariat who fought, not the Jewish intelligentsia.

The situation of the Jews, especially of the young men and women who graduated from colleges, was hopeless. They saw there was no future, no life, nothing to hope for. There were many very gifted young people. Religiously, they were disliked, socially, they were not accepted, and economically they were very much discriminated against. They couldn't find jobs. They wouldn't be accepted to work in a factory. They wouldn't be accepted as white-collar workers in the big concerns or big commercial plants. So really all they could do was to have little shops or just work as seamstresses, tailors, or maybe in sweat shops. They were not absorbed into the economy because they were discriminated against as Jews.

Unfortunately the Poles didn't understand that this was a loss for the Polish economy. I must say that in addition to the situation described, there were many Poles, who had cordial relations with Jews, showed them love not only before the war, but also during the German occupation. Some risked their lives to save a Jew, and a number of those even lost their lives. I personally had a number of good Polish friends.

There was a great resentment, and this went on from day to day, from month to month, from year to year. There were some young men and women who understood that they had to change the situation. There were actually two channels, both very much extreme. One group joined the Zionist old dream, feeling that if there were a Jewish state established, it would solve their critical situation. The immigration to Palestine during this period was limited by the fact that Palestine was under a British mandate. The controls were very strict. You had to have money too. There was a White Paper in 1937 which put down a quota, I believe, of 20,000. Also there was a monetary minimum that one had to declare on entering the country. As a result of this, those who did not possess this minimum could not come in, particularly the young, who were very actively working for the Zionist cause. If the immigration had been completely open to Palestine, there would have been a tremendous exodus. Thousands upon thousands would have gone and been saved. They were in the hopeless situation of growing up into adulthood and not being able to find a place in the society.

Immigrating to other countries to fill the quotas allotted to England and the United States, among others, was very hard. Nobody would accept Jews in the quotas of Poles. There were no quotas to England from Poland. There was a small quota for the United States. Very singular cases could go to Canada and to the dominions. You couldn't go to Italy and France. Most of the young people were not really interested in emigrating. They felt that they were in their own country and they felt a strong family bond. They did not want to leave the family. They would, however, have gone to Palestine, if they had had the means and if they had been allowed. To go to Palestine you had to be really young and strong, not only morally but physically too. The economic situation in Palestine was very critical. The young people could toil in a *Kibbutz*, and this demanded idealism. At that time the Kibbutz was a collective farm and these were city boys and girls. So this was a complicated problem. There were many Zionists, among which were a religious party, and workers' parties. At that time Europe was in general known for the great abundance of political parties of different persuasions.

Some Poles and proportionally more Jews shared visions of social justice and of economical changes facing a great unemployment, inflation and fascistic trends in the government.

A very small number of young people gravitated toward communism, believing that a super-national country, a heaven for workers, would assure equality and tolerance for all its citizens, that everybody would work and everybody would be paid according to his merits. What a great disappointment awaited them with the invasion of Poland by Soviet Russia, when one social evil was replaced by another greater one.

This idea attracted a number of young people, because at that moment it seemed like the only solution of the working masses and of the Jewish question. But this was a very small minority. The idea had an attraction, because the young people thought that this way they would get jobs. They did not know yet about the practical, social trap, which became apparent later on.

The Polish state was anti-Communist. Anything that was national, and Zionism was national, had a great possibility to flourish. It was even sometimes supported by the government, whereas anything that was international, like international communism, was a danger to the government and, therefore, was suppressed. It was illegal. There was not too much attraction to the young Jewish community in Marxism, which at that time promised the needed bread and butter. The majority felt very patriotic and served in the Polish army, where there was complete equality, without segregation in the barracks or in other ways.

The Jewish losses on the battlefield in 1939 were respectively much greater than the general Polish losses, particularly in the war under Kutno, one of the biggest military campaigns in Poland during the seventeen days. There were a tremendous number of Jewish men who fell on the battlefield. In the place where my husband's brother perished, in the camps in Kozielsk-Katyn, thirty per cent of all officers taken as prisoners of war were Jewish, even though the Jews constituted only ten per cent of the general population.

In the Polish army the Jews were discriminated against as far as becoming higher officers. There were two generals, for example, one of whom was General Mundt, who had to accept Catholicism. They were hidden Jews like the "marranos," Jews who had to accept Christianity in Spain, remaining inwardly Jewish. On Yom Kippur, the holiest Jewish holiday of the year, they would come tacitly to a synagogue and pray, incognito of course, while they were publicly known as Catholics. As a soldier, the Jew was not discriminated against.

CHAPTER TWO

GERMANY INVADES POLAND (1939)

My older brother, the lawyer, was in the so-called category 'D', which meant that he would never be called to the army, even in the case of a mobilization. He was medically unfit. He had undergone several surgeries. My stepbrother, Stas, who was an engineer, was not in the country. He had left for New York to see the World's Fair. My third brother, Adam, the doctor, was not called. Shortly before the war started there was a premonition that something was going to happen. And we were really excited. We almost wanted war, to fight for freedom and against the German dictatorship. We were building antiaircraft and shelter trenches. We girls went to dig too. Everybody was assigned to play a role. There were a lot of old fortifications, built in case of war. In addition to the young people, older volunteers had signed up to dig trenches. The streets were full of trenches. On the first of September, when the war started, we looked up and saw the sky blackened with airplanes. Tension rose during the course of the day. This was a real war, which brought us excitement. We believed that our powerful Polish air force would destroy the attacker "in no time." We really believed it, but in no time, we were disappointed. The fabricated tales which began circulating about Polish victories evaporated. There were no newspapers and few people listened to foreign news on the radio. My mother and father were frantic. They remembered the tragic First World War and said, "This is it! This is war. What are we going to do?" It was depressing. We immediately started to feel the wartime living conditions with closed shops and markets, with dark streets after sundown and with public alerts. Every so often we heard military bulletins. The atmosphere was nerve-racking as we were told to watch for surprise German attacks and for spies.

On the fifth of September the order was given on the radio by the commander of the army, General Smigly-Rydz, for all young men and women to leave the city immediately. He planned to defend Warsaw. Maybe he thought this would be the fighting line and he wanted to save the population.

Our mood had sunk and we decided to pack our suitcases to leave town. The whole young civilian population was to move out, perhaps to be used again later as reserves and to save them somehow. The exodus of primarily young people started in an unorganized fashion. Some entire families with small children and some belongings took also to the road, in spite of the universal danger. The weather was fortunately nice and the summer was felt all around us. Warsaw was bombed with great intensity and fires engulfed the destroyed buildings, from which dead and wounded were carried out. Hundred of houses were turned into rubble.

With shattered nerves we said goodbye to our parents and we took small suitcases with us. My two brothers and I, in fear of the uncertainty, decided to join other young people, hoping that we would come back in two days. We could not imagine that we were entering the waters of no return. In the beginning we felt as if we were going for an outing.

Everybody was going towards the east. The Germans

were coming from the west. Our cousins also came from the west. They lived close to Silesia where my aunt was a dentist. Not being at their home, they felt lost.

We left Warsaw with knapsacks on our backs. On the way I met some friends who asked me if I was also coming. I could not understand what they thought. One could see the mass exodus. Everybody rushed toward the bridge of Kierbedzia. This led to Praga, a suburb of Warsaw. Air raids continued all the time. Just as we passed the bridge, a full-scale warning sounded, a big bang was heard and as we looked back, the other side, which connected it with Warsaw, was bombarded from the air. The explosion was shocking, the like of which we never experienced before. We caught our breath and we thought that in a while we would be done away with when a big explosion occurred nearby. We heard the humming of the German airplanes and more explosions. You could already see some homes damaged, but the main bombing happened a few days later. Even now, as we were going, we already saw big fires here and there and buildings going up in smoke. I just passed the area where I used to attend the school of Mrs. Lange. There was only smoke and blazing fires. Heat was radiating as we past that firestorm. Some of the damaged buildings had blown out windows and scratched away surfaces. The German air force attacked with overnight air raids, using incendiary bombs. We did not see yet any casualties, but the material damage was great. The view of some of the residential streets turned into piles of rubbish had a demoralizing effect on the refugees. In the deadly danger we had to wade through broken bricks, stone and glass. This was our first taste of the war. We saw an ambulance picking up a wounded person on a stretcher, while other victims surrounded by their families were waiting nearby. What we saw was enough and we asked when would the war be over anyway.

So we walked out of Praga going to the east. We were

driven by fear. The mass of humanity was following us. There were a few immobilized trains. We walked on the main highway, full of noise and honking sounds. You saw thousands of young people with packages. Nobody knew where to go and none of us seemed to know what the next hours would bring. As we walked, somebody was following us with machine guns. The German air force was strafing the roads. The airplanes used to fly very low and you could see the pilots—like stretching out your hand. They killed thousands of civilians. You couldn't bear it. We ducked to the side of the road whenever we saw an approaching enemy. You considered all the refugees on the road to be your friends and sometimes you just imagined that a passerby was a person you knew. You didn't have time to stop. In the beginning we made the mistake of traveling during the day. But very soon we decided to travel by night. We slept in stables. This was September, a time when it can be very cold in Poland. The peasant farmers were very good and very cooperative. It was hard because at night you really did not see well and did not know where you were going. It was like a nightmare. You were surrounded by noises and people talking. Everybody was rushing. We were tired and we couldn't go too far. When we left home, each one of us took a round loaf of bread and some fruits. We never realized the needs that we would have, hoping that we would be going back home very soon.

We did not have any money with us. We had it in the bank, but banks had blocked all accounts on the second day of the war. Only our cousin who came from the west had a little money. He had just graduated from law school. He joined up with us, since his mother and father had come to live with us after their town was occupied by the Germans. So when we left Warsaw there were six of us young people: my two brothers, my younger sister and I, two cousins, the lawyer and his younger sister. And then there were some friends.

My oldest sister was married and remained in Warsaw because she had little children. My older sister was in a little town not far from Bialystok, which was almost on the Russian border. She had her office there and had married a doctor. Her place was not too far from Warsaw. She had established herself as a dentist in 1938 and had a good practice.

Afraid that the Germans would overtake us soon, we were trying to go farther east The cousins bought some food and the peasants gave us a piece of meat or some eggs, whatever you could buy. We were so scared, so hard-pressed to get somewhere, that we really did not care too much for food. We ate once a day, usually whenever we were ready to sleep in a stable, of course first obtaining permission from the peasant farmers. We told them that we were refugees from Warsaw. They were very nice, wonderful people, and shared their meals with us. Then my cousin always gave them a token payment.

We didn't starve along the way. As I recall, I wasn't too hungry, but then, as we went further, things changed. The first place we came to was Falencia, a little resort village. It had a large Jewish population. Everybody was just running like crazy. The people were confused. We were surrounded by the noise of people and buzzing of flies. The people asked us, "Why did you come here? We can't help you." We told them that we didn't want anything from them and that we just wanted to be as far away as possible from the front lines. We did not stay there long. The atmosphere almost smelled with abnormal days ahead and the sun seemed to be more distant. But I remember that it was a very depressing sight. People took their belongings out in the street and seemed very confused. Somebody placed his belongings in a wooden shed in full view and disappeared.

We went farther until we came to Otwock, also a resort town. We stayed there two days. This resort was very well-known for its high medical qualities. It supposedly had very clean air, which attracted tuberculosis patients, especially children. We decided that it was a good place to stay for a while. As we arrived there was a fusillade. It was just awful. The area around us was surrounded by flames, which almost touched us in the narrow streets, and it looked as if the entire world was ablaze. Showers of sparks came close to our skin. This was the first time that we had really come very close to being exposed to bombing, because we were in the open field. We spread out, out of breath. The people were mostly walking on, following the road, but we just wanted to get to a house. While we were still in this field, when the bombing started by low flying German planes, we were shocked. It was a terrible feeling. It was, I imagine, just like someone is in an open field and there is thundering and a feeling that the thunder will hit you. The noise seemed to go through and through you. When a missile slammed closely, I was petrified and I can't forget this. I just clutched my brother and said, "Adam, if anything happens to me, just pray that I will be killed at once, without suffering." I was afraid that I would just get injured. I did not want to suffer. I wished to get away from this piercing, deafening sound of the bomb. Let it be finished. So I was just clinging to my brother. This lasted for quite a long time. We later found trenches, in which we hid. The whole country was a vast network of underground shelters and trenches. So we were fortunate. We came to a trench and there were already some other people from the spa. Maybe two or three bombs fell within just a few yards and created a big hole in our vicinity. Burning beams were protruding from the hit buildings. It took maybe ten or fifteen minutes before it was safe to pick up our heads. We had to dig out from the crater and we were all full of sand. There was no mud, just clear white sand. We had difficulty to believe that we were still alive. We went a little farther and everywhere we saw some casualties. There were shouts and yells because they couldn't organize the help immediately. There were many people crying and nobody could help them. It took time before help arrived. Ambulances and hospitals were disorganized. Some people took care of themselves and walked with bandages on their heads and extremities. As a matter of fact, when we went farther, there were some hospitals that had been bombed too. At that time they did not have the Red Cross, not in the beginning of the war.

Thoughts about mother and the rest of the family came to us. Were they still alive or had we lost them?

It was so sudden, a real *blitzkrieg*. Then we came to one of our most famous airports. We were very proud of our air force which had a very good record. The Polish pilots were wonderful. We thought that in case of war we were really going to have the edge over any enemy. Then we saw everything cut to pieces. They explained to us that the Germans had attacked on the second day of the war. They skipped Warsaw and many towns and all their efforts were concentrated in immobilizing all the airports. And we had maybe only three or four. This was their end—the big air force might of Poland was shattered. It was very depressing when we saw that our army was retreating in disorder and that there was nothing left.

When the war broke out, we were optimistic. We couldn't believe that this calamity could happen to us. We felt that Poland was very strong and didn't realize what a mighty enemy we faced. We still hoped. "There is one other element. We have mighty allies, England, America, and France, who won't let us down and will immediately declare war." We were praying. When they declared war, it was a little late and did not help much. This was our big illusion.

We had some family, my mother's sister, who lived in a good-sized town, Siedlce. We came there and thought that maybe in this town we could find some rest, because we were exhausted. It had been maybe four or five days since we left. The town was only about sixty miles away from Warsaw, but we felt it so far away. When we arrived there, everything was ablaze. Building after building was hit and burned out. It was just a pity to look at the town. You could see only the naked chimneys sticking out. I remember that I just cried. I lost the sense of time. We had to hide immediately, because you could hear a fusillade, and we did not know where it came from. It was so hard because The German Luftwaffe was attacking and at the same time the so-called *Volksdeutsche*, Poles, who had suddenly discovered that they were of German origin and felt that they had an obligation to protect and fight for their Fatherland, had started to attack ethnic Poles. We were caught in a crossfire at this time and decided to leave this place as soon as possible.

It was a very pitiful sight when we left the town. People were confused and sometimes behaved strangely, walking with their bundles aimlessly as if they were in an insane asylum. At one spot we passed scattered dead bodies, while on another we passed a destroyed car. A mother lost her child. Another person lost a mother. The tragedy was obvious and nobody knew where to go and what to do. We were very exhausted and weak. My girl cousin had trouble with her feet. We knew that the Germans were on 'our heels,' and that they were rapidly proceeding, because whenever we came to a place, Germans were not far from us.

In the beginning Warsaw was still holding out. It fell, I believe, on the seventeenth of the month, though there are some who say it was defending itself till the twenty-third of September. Our troubles grew worse since my cousin who was a young girl couldn't walk because her feet were blistered. Being very tired, we dropped all our belongings, including all the dresses and coats. In the beginning we had our little suitcases with these extra clothes. My sister took party dresses and a little evening gown. Now, we got rid of everything and we were 'free people.'

Nobody even thought about having a bath. We decided to go closer to the trains, hoping that maybe we would be able to hitch a ride. When we came closer to a train, it was full of soldiers. Nobody was permitted on the train but soldiers, who tried to joke with us. They were not too encouraging. They immediately told us to leave. A stream of people was with us on the road.

For a short time our boys carried the girl cousin. But they couldn't carry her far. We tried to flag down passing carriages, but nobody paid any attention to our efforts. Therefore, dead tired and hungry, we had to make a stop for a day and we stayed on a farm.

The next day we found an empty house. It was abandoned and partially bombed. We were looking for food and found some. The people had disappeared in the midst of eating. We just finished their left-over meal. We were so delighted that we did not have to beg or ask anybody. We washed ourselves in this place because we were not rushed for time. We were glad we had found this little oasis and we felt as if we were in our own home. But it was not much of a hiding place. We left in the evening and took a little food with us. We felt encouraged, perked up and fairly well rested.

Then came a night that I will never forget. We were on the main road, on which so much was going on, while we passed soldiers, civilians, men and women. People were walking in different directions as the moon shone brightly. I couldn't figure out what was going on. I now realize that we were on the main road. From time to time you could see some carriages passing by and maybe once in a while a car. A car was very exotic at that time. As we saw a few carriages, we approached them asking for a ride. People were hanging over a carriage, perhaps twenty people on a vehicle, as long as the horse was pulling them. The night and confusion brought us a tragic surprise. As we approached the carriages, we discovered that we had lost our brother, the doctor. It happened that, as we talked to the driver, we lost Adam in the streaming crowd. We looked all over but couldn't find him.

The night became a nightmare closing in around us. People were going in different directions. It was just like a big madhouse. We prayed that the confusion would end and that we would get some solution, because we did not know what to do with ourselves. At dawn we realized that we would not be able to find my brother. I felt a sudden panic deprived his protection. We asked every passerby about him. Some people told us that they had seen him not far from the main road and that he had joined an army unit. We understood that the people, trying to get rid of us, lied. Later a rumor spread that the war was almost over. We did not believe that this was possible but we were willing to accept it. We assumed that Adam was safe and we decided to make the best of things. We started on our way at the light of the moon, surrounded by the silhouettes of the marching refugees and their shadows.

Two days later, as we were going farther on the road, the airplanes were again over flying very low. Some of them were bombing and the others were using machine guns. The pilots saw us and knew that we were a civilian population. We tried to duck. In some places we entered a little forests and there were small bushes behind which we could hide but on most of the road there was no cover. During late afternoon the murmur of the German airplanes became almost uninterrupted.

In ten days, during which the outcome of the war was still unclear, German tank divisions were moving deep into Poland and it was all over. Many young Jews perished on the battlefield. Others, like we, left their families, businesses and professions, their burning homes, and ran east.

CHAPTER THREE

RUSSIAN OCCUPATION

Contact with Russians at Rozyszcze in the Ukraine

After a few days we finally came to a town called Rozyszcze in the Ukraine. Geographically this part was called Volhynia, or in Polish, Wolyn. When we came there the place was quiet and peaceful. We decided that we would not go any farther and that we would stay there and get a good rest. The people in this town were very friendly and there was a considerable number of Jews, who were wonderful and helpful. They gave us a little home and clothes, which we badly needed, some food, and moral support. We felt very lucky to be there, in particular since the town must have been overburdened with thousands of people.

In every tragedy you can find little light moments. There were many people that we knew before, but could not meet in the big city of Warsaw. You never dreamt that you would ever bump into them and here in this small town we met them. They were old acquaintances, friends of my brothers and sisters. So I wound up knowing quite a number of people in town.

We spent two days in that town and our acute fears disappeared. We decided to relax and to wait and see.

Suddenly, one night our peace was disturbed. Something was going on—people were walking in the streets fearing that the unexpected was going to happen. There was an aura of an unknown mystery in the air. Everybody sort of felt this way. Somebody suddenly came with the news that the Russians were coming. We had never seen a Russian and didn't know what Russians were like. We really would have to admit that we probably thought they were barbarians. We never knew anything about them. We were very scared. Poles hated the Russians. This is inculcated in Polish upbringing. We were afraid that they were going to kill us right away and we were pleasantly surprised when the Russians announced on the radio that they came as brothers and that they were going to liberate us from the oppression of the Germans and that they were against war.

Many more Jews than Poles shared visions of brotherhood and social justice, promised by a socialistic regime. We wished that our social dreams would come through. The reality brought us a great disappointment. The Russian army penetrated into the territories of western Ukraine and western White Russia. We couldn't figure it all out. If they were against the war, why had they occupied our territory? But the expressions which they used—that they were coming to liberate us—was baffling, but did not quiet our fears.

We did not know what to do. We were trapped. There was no way to go back, because on the other side were the Germans. We were afraid of the war—of the fire, the guns and the bombs. We knew that only the Russian talk was friendly and that they were going to do something to us. We did not know what to expect. One felt just like digging a little hole in the ground and disappearing. All the time we were going east because we thought that the east would be spared—that the Polish army would stop the Germans so we could return home. Not knowing what to expect from the Russians, we were fearful of the unknown element, but the older folks in town, who had previously known the Russians, started to tell us not to be afraid—that they were people, friendly like everybody else, and wouldn't harm us.

They came the next day. But the feeling was just like in a séance. We felt lifeless and did not know how to act. We waited for the worst to happen. When the Russian troops entered town they were under good control and discipline and they gave a big parade. They were going to the front with their tanks and other military equipment. They told the people in the streets that all would be well and they gave us sausages and cheeses. You detected an effort to gain our confidence. We did not say much and we were even afraid to eat what they gave us, thinking perhaps the food was poisoned. Some of them started to kiss us, stating that now we were free and that here was no more war. We couldn't believe what they told us. The day brought us an unbelievable turn of events. It did not take long to recognize the violent fist of the dictatorship.

Suddenly their tone changed. They claimed that there were some remnants of the Polish army that were hostile to them and they were shooting at the Russian soldiers. Now, when they were marching through the main street, they were shooting in the air in all directions from their tanks. We were in a small little home. The windows had shutters and we could see the shooting through the windows. When they were shooting, it was just like somebody had turned on the electricity in the whole house. It went on all night long. We were really in a panic. They just went on a rampage.

We left the main room and went to the hall, where there were no windows, returning every so often to peep out. We were very scared and could hear only our heartbeat. It was very dangerous. Many people were killed the following night. The shooting did not stop till daybreak. Since on the first day they gave out the food and talked about liberation and on the second day they did the shooting, they apparently got little resistance from Polish patriots. Sporadically, individuals took shots at the Russians. There weren't organized units around. The Polish people had a wonderful tradition. They were fearless. They had a big disregard for their own safety and life, when it came to their country. They used to say: "*Salus rei publicae suprema lex esto.*" ("The good of the country is above all."). It is difficult to find such great devotion and loyalty in other countries.

Finally the Russians cleared the town and continued on their way. Then came the Russian civil administration. Everywhere they planted a few people to run the local government. In the beginning they tried not to alienate the local population. Some people co-operated with the invaders because they wanted to make a go of it. Within a few days, other people were detained by the Russians. They took the upper strata of the society, the very rich people, and the people who had a record of being anti-Communist. They gathered information from local Communists. The illegal refugees and local merchants were deported inside Russia. Registration was strictly followed and violators were severely punished. After a few days of disorders and anxiety, life started to stabilize. I didn't know what I could do in this little town. After the rest, I left my family and went to Lvov on a train with no trouble.

When the Russians came we did not have any money. In order to support us, my brother, Henry, the lawyer, decided to find work. He went to the depot in the morning and found a job loading coal into the cars. He worked the whole day and came home in the evening with a high fever. He had not been well, although he was pretty strong. Before the war he had malaria, which was spread by a mosquito in marshes of eastern Poland. With regard to his legal matters he had gone to a place that was swampy. He was ill for a few months. We were scared when he came home with a high fever, close to 106 degrees at one point. Now, within three or four days he had recovered.

Since he could not do physical work, I advised him to try to get a teaching job. He got a job in an elementary school, teaching arithmetic and geography. Now, I decided to leave him and go to Lvov to attend the university.

CHAPTER FOUR

ATTENDING THE UNIVERSITY OF LVOV

During the war one could board a train very easily due to the total disarray. There were no fixed hours of departure, and sometimes they were eight or twelve hours late. You just waited. So many people with their belongings were waiting around the train. You did not have to have any documents or tickets to buy. When I came to Lvov in October 1939, I was very pleased. I decided to attend the university and to finish my studies. I did not have any friends or relatives there. By chance I met on the train the husband of a cousin of mine, whom I had never seen before. This man was a very prominent man, a Congressman. He also was a very active Zionist. So the Nazis and the Russians were after him. During the war he has come to Lvov where his father lived. I knew about him, but I really had never met him before. He was a society man, very rich. He was very nice and he gave me his address. He said that if I needed any help I should call him. I took the address and was glad that at least I knew somebody. I wasn't sure that I was going to use it, but one never knew.

After I got off the train at Lvov, I did not know really what to do with myself. I had no money. I hoped that maybe I would be able to enroll in the university. At the university I met some friends whom I had known as students at the University of Warsaw. They informed me that I could live at the beautiful university dormitories. If you were a student in a Russian university, you were automatically assigned to a dormitory and you would get room and board and pocket money. I had no papers, but I had witnesses that I had studied.

Lvov was in Poland before the war. Now it was under the Russians. The university was operating. This was an unusual situation and they were willing to help whoever was willing to study. We had many of the old teachers. They assigned me to a dormitory, which was very fancy. There were three girls in a room. For the first time I slept in a clean room. It was wonderful. Everything was taken care of—no more worries. When we came to school everybody got paid his expenses for the entire month. I was very happy. We were going to school and working.

We soon learned that there was a shortage of food. One could barely make it on the food they gave us. It consisted of soup with a slice of bread. There was no meat. There were some beans and cooked carrots. In the beginning everything looked nice and rosy, but later we saw that some rooms did not have windows and in other rooms the heating system was broken down. The winter in Lvov was very severe. Not having enough clothing to wear, we were shivering and freezing. I was cold and undernourished. Gloomy days with severe frost plus hungry stomachs caused around me scenes of despair. Pretty soon the romance was over. We started to show our disappointment and we notified the authorities that things called for improvement, but they did not respond and got very mad. They told us, that instead of being pleased with what they were doing for us we were complaining, but when they were going to school, in 1918-19, they were much worse off than we. We did not make any headway with them. The university administration had been taken over by the Russians, but the teachers were the same as before the war.

I was there a few months. One day I was called to the administration and told that they were sorry but they couldn't continue giving me my scholarship in the form of the subsidy that they gave. When I asked what was the reason for it, and was I not making the grades, they explained that they were not concerned with this, but that they were told that I was a *kulak*, a rich member of the society. I was frantic and when I asked on what basis I was being accused, they told me that they learned that my uncle was fabulously rich. They asked whether this was true. When I answered in the affirmative, they said threateningly, that I am "a member of a bad family." At that time Jewish businessmen and political activists were arrested and deported by the Soviets.

I tried to explain that he was a brother of my father and that I had nothing in common with him. He had never shown any interest in us. He knew that his youngest brother had died and had left a young widow with three children but he was indifferent. I had never even met him. They did not want to accept my explanation, because I was from a rich family. I felt extremely depressed. I did not know what I am going to do since I had no means to support myself. The authorities probably found out about this from some students who knew my name and somehow connected me with my uncle. There were some communists who felt that the day had come for revenge. They did not have anything against me personally but they associated my name with my uncle and they decided to report me and thus to show the Russian administration their eagerness to perform a good political job.

They simply took away my scholarship and I had to leave the dormitory. When I left, I learned that you could not live without a passport, a document which identified you everywhere you went. One could not even sleep in a place without having these documents. I was disappointed with this political system. I felt degraded and I decided to go back to Warsaw, to the German side, and to be with my parents, even though I read about German victories in France. At that moment I did not think that the war would drag on. I went to register in order to be able to get back.

If my application were approved, I would have to cross the river San and go to Przemysl, a border town divided by the two occupying powers into two zones, and from there I would go back home. That entire area was in turmoil. I received one or two letters from home. My mother wrote me to come home where all would be arranged and okay. She was afraid that we were helpless and she thought that she could use her ingenuity to help us. Despite her having suffered a lot, as I found out after the war, she wrote me how things were good. And I wrote her that things were good with us, because I didn't want to worry her.

I could not trust the Russians. They told us that, whoever was from the German side, could easily go back home. I changed my name when I registered with the Russians. I now used the name of my stepfather, which I had never accepted officially. I used this maneuver only to be permitted to leave in safety.

CHAPTER FIVE

LIVING IN LVOV AFTER EJECTION FROM THE UNIVERSITY

Providence was wonderful to me. While I was walking in my predicament down the street, I suddenly bumped into a boy who was a very good friend of mine and in love with me back home, in Warsaw. He was so happy and delighted to see me and he comforted me after he heard my story. His name was Janek. It was surprising how many people I met in Lvov whom I had known in Warsaw and who, I was sure, were lost. Janek was very happy and invited me to stay with his family. When he learned that I didn't have a passport, he promised to help me.

His family lived in a large room. There were maybe five or six people. You were not allowed to live in any home without a permit. Each home had a concierge, who watched who entered the house and was spying for the police. Janek warned me to be careful and brought me some of his clothes. I got dressed as a boy and entered the house at night. The concierge did not see me, but if he had, Janek would have told him that I was his friend. He brought me clothes so I could change somewhere else. He worked and had money, some of which he gave me. He provided me with some papers, which enabled me to enroll in another school. I left the house dressed also as a boy.

At first in the new school they gave everybody scholarships, but later you had to earn it, getting good grades in all subjects. They also gave out loans to people who needed them. I enrolled in two schools because I wanted to be very safe. I hoped to get some financial support in either school.

On the campus of the university you could live without a passport, while elsewhere you couldn't. The bulk of the student body were refugees from the west. They didn't have roots in this city and immediate area. The Russians looked upon us with suspicion. They did not trust us at all. They considered us as counter-revolutionary, an unreliable foreign element. The local students knew how to manage their lives—how to find clothes and food. But we were just alien to everything and there was nobody to help us. The Russians promised that they were going to give us passports and that as long as we were in the colleges we didn't need them.

All colleges were state-run. I went to a polytechnic during the day, studying mechanical engineering. At night I attended a library college with emphasis on how to run libraries. I had a lot of fun studying. I worked very hard, although I did not have much to eat.

In the meantime I received letters from my brother, Henry, who worked as a teacher in Rozyszcze receiving a small salary. My little sister, Zosia, came to Lvov, but she left immediately. She was traveling from town to town searching for a proper job. She finally settled with my older sister, Basia, who married in 1939, before the war broke out and lived near Bialystok. She stayed with her only about a week or a little more and got homesick. Since Basia's home was eleven or twelve kilometers from the border, one day Zosia crossed the border on the way to Warsaw, without saying a word to her older sister, or without leaving a letter. Basia and my brother-in-law were frantically looking for her. They did not know how she had suddenly disappeared.

The Russians had promised us all along that we were going to get passports, but we were tense, sensing that something wrong was being prepared for us. I lived in a small dormitory on the second floor. One night, I was awakened from my sleep by voices and shots. My windows faced a little court. So I went across the hall to another room facing the street. I moved as quietly as I could. I felt as though the ceiling were falling on my head. I saw two very long, low ladder-wagon containing two Russian soldiers with rifles, on both sides of each. They were forcing students, who didn't want to go, to climb up unto the wagons. Some students cried.

Other students were asleep. I had only seconds to contact others. It was difficult to make my way in the darkness. I was tormented because I didn't know whether I should wake everyone up, but the fear prevailed and I jumped from the window. I was scared. The gate in the back was locked and the concierge had closed also the front door for the night. I concealed myself in a dark corner. My heart was pounding and I was very frightened. I soon understood that the Russians had come to deport the students who did not have papers. Some students were from nearby, from the Russian-occupied zone. They were really refugees without papers. I was one of them. They did not detect me. They probably thought that they would get me later and in the meantime they went on to look for illegal students in the other buildings. That night taught me a lesson about the Russian love of the downtrodden.

The terrain burned under my feet and the next day I decided to leave in a hurry. Since it was dangerous to walk the streets without having papers, I went back to my friend and asked him for help.

The following night I went to the college and spent the night in a huge classroom. I decided that, since I could not hide anymore, I would leave Lvov and go to my brother.

In the meantime, I had gotten news from my mother that my brother Adam was in Lithuania and that he was well off, working as a physician. I tried to figure out how to get to him. Janek promised me some help, but I had to do it all on my own. I had no detailed plan and for a few nights I just hid, going from one friend to another.

In the meantime, we kept hearing that the Russians were taking people and sending them to Siberia, to Archangelsk. They deported my cousin and his sister. I couldn't get to my brother and I also couldn't obtain official papers. For quite a while the Russians had been circulating notices on the billboards that there were people needed in many towns. They listed Crimea, Tashkent, and the best places you could think of. This was similar to the dream of immigrants to the States, dreaming about California. I knew that the Russians would not give me papers because I was considered a refugee and I decided that I would enroll in the list of volunteers going to Russia.

This was a special policy of the Bolsheviks to get rid of the people, whom they did not trust in the new territories and at the same time to get cheap labor deep in Russia. The queue of people volunteering to go to Russia grew longer. We gathered and they gave everybody two loaves of bread. I looked around to see what kind of people registered. They were old and sick looking people. I did not see any young people. I realized that this element was not acceptable for work and I couldn't figure out what the Russians were planning to do with those people. I decided that I did not fit in this group and I decided I had better stay on the Polish soil. I put my towel over my neck and went to wash myself. This was at the depot where there were very many trains. There were no separate spaces for the civilian population and for the soldiers. One had to orient oneself quickly to change plans. Even though I felt helpless, I quickly decided what to do. When I went to wash myself outside the gate, I did not return to my previous place, but

I went farther and farther. I started running in the direction of the train, which began to move toward Russia after ten minutes. I left my bread and belongings behind and I disappeared.

They had already taken down my name, but there was a melee. They had so many names that they could never count the people. The groups were in constant flux. After the registration, some people would change the destination in Russia and move to other groups. People did not know much about the geography of places where they volunteered to go.

I would like to add at this time that many Jews who went to Russia at that time, as I originally had wanted to, survived the war. I could have survived easily by going to Russia without experiencing the hell of the camps. Many succumbed in Russia, but they were not exposed to the atrocities of the Germans. They starved to death, but generally, if they were young and vigorous, they made it. And many Jewish boys later entered the Red Army and fought the Germans. Then, when they were demilitarized, they again became Polish citizens or Rumanian citizens and so forth.

I experienced a feeling of relief, a relaxation of fear and tension. This was my second escape from the Russians. The first was when I did not go with them when they were taking the people without passports. The fear I had that the Russians would deport me at that moment, were quieted.

I don't think the Russians actually sent the volunteers to places where they wanted to go. The rumor was that those people were used to perform slave labor. At the end of the war many Polish Jews found themselves in Uzbekistan and deep in Asia. But in the beginning Jews, Poles, and other refugees were sent into the forced labor camps in Wologda and Archangelsk, close to the White Sea, and in Donbas, close to the Black Sea. It wasn't a worker's paradise at all. However, you could survive if you were strong. I was very exhausted, very weak, had no stamina, and I wanted to stay in Poland, closer to my family.

CHAPTER SIX

VILNO, LITHUANIA (JANUARY 1941)

I decided to go to Vilno, Lithuania, where my brother, Adam, was. He had written me that he was fairly well off there. He had a very good job in a hospital, working as a general practitioner and he was also an assistant professor of medicine. He came to Vilno in 1939 after we had lost him in the heavy traffic in the flight from Warsaw.

It wasn't easy to get to him because the distance from Lvov to Vilno was many hundred of kilometers. There was a borderline between Lithuania and Poland, but the international relations between the two countries were not too well organized and both countries were under Soviet domination. One had to deal with the Russians. I started out hitchhiking. The route took me through several stations to my destination and after a long time I finally managed to reach Vilno, where I met Adam with a joyful emotion. He welcomed me with kisses and was happy that I made it to him.

I saw quite a big difference between Lithuania and Poland. Lithuania was much better off economically. Lithuania had special stores, so-called *Mestas*, where you could buy all the meat products, all the dairy products and other items. The windows were full of food on display. They were occupied but this was a special policy of the Soviets, not to alienate the Lithuanians, and to give them the feeling of security. And that's what they did in the first phase of the war. They treated all the Baltic countries, Lithuania, Estonia, and Latvia, quite favorably.

I didn't have any money and I could not buy all these products. I decided to get a job, but jobs were scarce. There were not too many refugees at that time from west or south Poland that I might meet. When I came to Vilno, I was told that the entire traffic of refugees stopped in December 1940, that some of them had boarded ships and had gone away—some to Denmark, Holland, China, or to the Middle East. This traffic was illegal. I was familiar with the lot of some non-Jews. I understood that some of the richer Lithuanians had been taken by the Russian government and sent deep into Russia and Siberia.

The illegal emigration of the Jews was sponsored by the Zionist organization, which was interested in saving Jewish lives, especially of the people who were prominent in the political and social life before the war. They saved them from both sides, from the Russians and from the Germans. I felt that it was just the people who were prominent before the war who were given priority in being able to emigrate while the little fellow couldn't save himself that easily, because the enemy first attacked the prominent citizens. The prominent people could also render their services to society in the future. There were some people with money who could afford to rent little ships privately. I don't know exactly to what extent illegal traffic took place, but some people did find a haven in other European countries or in the Far East, because they had the means.

Oddly enough, in Vilno, everything was still abundant and the Russians didn't remove all the goods as they used to do in occupied countries of the west Ukraine. This was January of 1941. There was a special policy of Soviet Russia not to alienate the Baltic countries and to give them a free hand to a certain extent. One of the aspects of this policy was not to deprive them of their food. The Lithuanians were big eaters.

Later, the Lithuanians, at least those who were cooperating with the Germans, took a very unfriendly view of the Jews. At the time of my arrival in Lithuania the relationship of the Lithuanians to the Jews was not bad. My first impression was that the Lithuanians were not on the side of the Communists They tried to preserve their institutions as much as they could. They had a very close relationship and kinship with other Lithuanians, but also courted the Poles who were, however, not treated on par with the Lithuanians. There wasn't any particular ill behavior as far as the Jews went. The Jewish question was not as acute at that time as it became later.

There was a very large Jewish community in Vilno before the war. Before the outbreak of the war, Vilno (Vilnius in English) was in the hands of the Poles and was considered very much a Polish town. The Poles gave the Jews great freedom and the Jews had a very progressive cultural life there. They had very good theaters, libraries, an active cultural life, and their religious life was protected. The rest of the Polish Jews were not in the same fortunate position. The Poles wanted to play the Jews against the Lithuanians and that is why they gave them more favorable treatment and why Vilno was the haven of the cultural Jews. They produced here very intelligent and talented people. Their schools were well-developed and Jewish culture flourished. This would lead to some avidity and the Lithuanians were envious of Jews and disliked them because of this favorable treatment.

When Soviet Russia entered the picture, they tried to get the sympathy of the population. When they occupied the three Baltic countries in 1940, they announced that they had come to free the oppressed people of Lithuania, and that Vilno was always a Lithuanian town. They implanted hatred into the Lithuanians against the Poles.

There were two segments of the Lithuanian population. One segment, a minority, were staunch Communists who went along with Soviet Russia and felt that the Russians would not go for any nonsense. So they tried to be liberal toward all nationalities and tried to defend the equality of all. Their attitude toward the Jews was positive, because they knew that Soviet Russia would not permit any discriminatory policy. The other group, the majority of Lithuanians, was strongly nationalistic, and as such, tried to discriminate against Jews. The Lithuanians were to a certain extent more nationalistic-minded than the Poles and they were also more anti-Russian than the Poles.

We did not come in social contact with them too much. During the first phase of the war the Lithuanians still enjoyed a fairly good standard of living. They had their jobs. Some of them maybe had to change jobs, but they still had a decent income. They were not friendly to us. The Poles knew us better and they would have more understanding. We spoke Polish and not the Lithuanian language. For that reason the relationship of the Lithuanians to the Lithuanian Jews was better than to us. It might be that they treated them as well as the Poles treated Polish Jews.

CHAPTER SEVEN

LATVIA

In February of 1941, my brother encouraged me to go to Latvia, where our family lived in the town of Daugavpils. This town is called Dvinsk in Russian. I thought that maybe I would feel better being with my family, because for so long I had been away from my relatives. I hoped to get warmth and understanding there. I was hungry for a good, normal family life. I knew from before the war that this part of my father's family was quite well off. This was my uncle, my father's brother, and cousins and they were very prominent in the town. My cousin was a known attorney—she was a district attorney. A friend of mine joined me on that journey. The road was very dangerous, and I will never forget how we had to steal over the border. We went on the train to the border town of Taurogi. This was the last stop and then there were many miles of flat land, stones and dunes on the no-man's land between the border lines. We decided to go on our own, being afraid to tell anybody where we were going.

When we crossed the border, beating frost and fear, we were soon stopped by the Soviet police and asked where we were going. We lied and said that we were looking for our father. The policemen started to examine us and brought us to a small room at the railroad station, where we saw quite a number of other people they were investigating. We spent part of one day and one night there. On the morning of the next day, as we were fighting off panic, they decided to let us go, saying, "Okay, you can go. We don't want to see you here any more, or else." Terrified, I was very much determined to reach my uncle and aunt and I decided, in spite of this warning, to go ahead with my plans. I couldn't believe that my family would not help me in this critical time. I started to run as long as I could.

Thereafter, we moved at night, not daring to travel during the day and we came again to a little place very close to the border. We told Lithuanian peasants that we had family in Latvia and paid them to take us on a sled. We were shivering in the cold, biting frost and we traveled for six and a half hours, mostly through the silent forest which finally brought us at the other side. We paid the peasants for their service. They were very friendly and nice to us. They even gave us something to eat.

When we came to the Latvian side we felt more secure. After some time we arrived in the town of Daugavpils. The reception by our family was very cold. They couldn't understand how we had come to them. They asked us, "How could you come here illegally?" I answered, "We came here because we wanted to see you. We understand that last year you told my brother, Adam, that you would like to see me and to take care of me." But, I remember their tense faces. They were very scared and said that there was nothing of this kind and this visit wasn't getting us anywhere. They told us how many prominent people were sent deep into Russia and that they were all living in terror. I knew that they were well off before the war. They had quite a large estate, but everything had been taken away from them, and they now lived in a very small house and had very modest means. I noticed that the house was partly bare. There were some knick-knacks and bric-a-brac, they probably had gathered from their previous home. My cousin told me that she had no more connections with the courts and that she was very much afraid not knowing what to do with me.

I felt a great coolness on their part, and their fear of the new regime was palpable. I did not see much point in hanging around and I decided to leave them. All of my big hopes to stay with them and to find a warm home dwindled. I saw that there was no room for me there and that I would be better off with my brother in Vilno.

On the third day I started off. They gave me some cookies, which I refused to take. Again I had to cross the border. I decided not to cross the border in the same place where I had passed before. I came to a little town and I started to get oriented in the geography of the place. People told me that I was very close to the border. They asked who I was and what I was looking for. I told them that I was from Lithuania.

I started to go to the border through a little forest and then through an empty field where there was a small barbed wire fence, which I did not see. It alerted the Russian guards who spotted me in the darkness. They brought me to their little station, and suddenly I found myself petrified in the same place where I had been a few days before and with the same people. There were three men, who were very puzzled as to why I was so stubborn and stayed in the neighborhood. They were steaming with anger and started to talk to me in an abusive sharp manner. They suspected that I must be a spy. I got very scared and started to cry. They talked to me in very highly pitched voices. They were cursing, sure that I was a criminal. I kept on saying that all I wanted was to find my lost relatives and that I had not found them. I had promised them to go back to Lithuania. I was finally told that my fate would be decided the next morning.

I spent a very bad night. Early in the morning, at 6:00 o'clock, I was called for a further interrogation. They brought me into a different room, where I faced two men. They told me that they would soon tell me what they would do. Asked different questions, I answered through the tears that I had not wanted to do anything wrong, but had just wanted to find my relatives. Finally they sent me back to the waiting room, where there were other people. One of them came close to me and asked if I knew what they did with spies. I said, "What?" He said, "They give them a death sentence." So again I started to cry. They did not know what to do with me. I kept saying that I was not politically minded and that all I wanted was to find a home. This was my tune all the time. I told them immediately that I was Jewish, but I don't think that there was a Jewish officer whose opinion could prevail under the situation. I also don't think that they were friendly toward Jews, because when they learned that I was a Jewish refugee, they could have let me go. I think that the truth prevailed. They realized that I just didn't have anything to do with politics. They did not know what to do with me. There were many smugglers on the border and the police were mainly busy apprehending them.

During the lunch the policemen gave me something to eat. They kept me in a small room next to the court. This was probably a detention room. The next day they told me to go, that I was very lucky, and they warned me not to come this way any more. I was very happy to regain my freedom.

The policemen on horses escorted us at night to a railroad station, where we boarded a train, and went back to Vilno. The town was brewing with new changes. We noted that the stores were not so full of goods as in the beginning, when we came there the first time.

CHAPTER EIGHT

WORKING IN VILNO

I got a job washing bottles in a big factory, and it wasn't easy since I had never done similar work before. Then I changed to a job as a waitress in a restaurant. I had also never been a waitress previously and it was quite a new experience. The reason why I took this job was simply hunger. I felt that I would be fed on the spot and that there would always be some leftovers which I could bring home to share with my brother and some close friends. The restaurant wasn't fancy, but it fed quite a number of people. Sometimes maybe fifty customers came to a dinner. There were a lot of dishes to wash. Not being skilled in this job, one day I fell and broke quite a number of dishes. This meant the end of my career as a waitress.

Finally, I got a job in the kitchen connected with Vilno University. They used to serve dinners for up to eight hundred students. I felt very fortunate to get this full-time job. The work started in the wee hours of the night and lasted until four o'clock p.m. It was winter and very cold. I went to work very early. We peeled potatoes and carrots, ground meat, and did the other necessary preparations. There usually was a foreman overseeing our work and always telling us to speed up. I knew that I was not too skilled in this line, but I tried to do my best. I was told that under no circumstances were we permitted to take any food home. In spite of this I tried on a few occasions to sneak out some food, especially bread and butter, which were freely distributed for the guests, and brought it home.

In the beginning the job seemed very pleasant, but I soon realized that I was not doing too well. The other girls had a lot in common. They spoke Lithuanian. Pretty soon they found out that I was Polish and they started to discriminate against me. They did not know anything about my being Jewish. If they had known that I was a Polish Jew rather than just Polish, they would have definitely treated me much worse. I worked there for quite some time. Almost daily, we had to grate potatoes and carrots. You had to do it manually. I cut my fingers and they were constantly bleeding. Very often I was grating the food and the blood was dripping, but I was afraid to take care of the wounds during work, because the foreman would fire me. On the other hand, because this took place every day, my fingers never could heal properly.

My coworkers in the kitchen noticed that I was silent and did not participate too much in their conversations. They thought that I maybe had an edge over them and wanted to demonstrate my superiority to them. They started to investigate my background. All they could find out was that I was educated, which brought many laughs and another wave of discrimination. They couldn't understand how I could work in that place and put up with the existing conditions.

I made an observation that the Lithuanians had a great appetite and could eat a lot. Sometimes they used to have from eight to ten main courses—course after course, almost five entrees with five additional smaller ones. They ate a little and left some. Whatever was not touched by the customers the waitresses washed up and ate, or brought home with them.

Since the Lithuanians ate so much, they looked very

sturdy. Oddly enough, they were not even overweight, but they were very well built, tall, and muscular. They lived well and they worked efficiently. They had an entirely different way of life than the Poles under Russian occupation.

The conditions worsened and I finally lost my job. I felt very bad. The discrimination against the Jews became greater and we had difficulty getting jobs. Even my brother, who was working at the hospital, noticed the change. The working conditions deteriorated and there was a feeling that some political changes were going to happen. The Russians occupied the high positions and we were just small pawns. I went to work at night and rushed home in the cold and sleet just to have enough time to eat and wash and to prepare myself for the next day. I could not afford to buy clothes and I had to live with the few little frocks that I had—some cotton dresses.

When I lost my employment, the situation became hopeless. At that time, I felt the resentment of the Lithuanians and I felt lost with nothing much that I could do. My brother, who was a very industrious man, decided to help me find a good job. He went to the Minister (Secretary) of Education, who at that time was a very prominent writer, and had made a great contribution to literature and poetry. He was a man who was loved by the entire Lithuanian population. Before the Second World War he authored many books and established for himself a name and position in the Lithuanian literature. He was very humane and gentle. When he met me he immediately assessed the situation. He felt very sorry that I had been so badly treated by his co-patriots, intelligent people with degrees, who felt free to discriminate.

I attended a school for two weeks to learn Lithuanian and I did very well. The teacher said that she had never met anyone who had learned to speak this language so quickly and so well in such a short time. She told me I would very quickly speak it fairly well. But when I later got a job I couldn't attend classes any more. I saw the Minister of Education two or three times in order to get a job. He was very gentle and affectionate. I felt very embarrassed when he kissed my hand. He told me: "This is awful that we Lithuanians treat people this way, and especially you." He gave me a lot of moral support and said that I should do what I was equipped for. He found a school where I could start teaching. It was April of 1941. I taught students at the seventh grade level. The class consisted of Polish children, whom I had to teach in Polish, which was easy for me. The other teachers taught the children Russian and Lithuanian. The kids were very cooperative and I really enjoyed my job. I taught math, literature, beginning of physics, and botany till June, when they went on vacation. I now had some money and the future was not as bleak as before.

CHAPTER NINE

GERMANY OCCUPIES VILNO (JUNE 22, 1941)

In June, shortly after school was over, we received a letter from our mother telling us about the great celebration coming up on June 22nd—our youngest sister was going to get married. We were in a festive mood and decided to celebrate at home. It was Saturday and we looked forward to Sunday because this was the wedding day. I couldn't understand why Zosia decided to get married at the young age of sixteen. I went to a store and got some alcohol and a homemade cake. Sunday morning we were glued to the radio and suddenly heard the voice of Molotov, who was not well known to us then, announcing that the German military had crossed the border between the Russian and German occupation zones of Poland. This meant war. Thus, the 22nd of June became a memorable date for us. The first phase of war had started on September 1, 1939, and this was the beginning of the second. From this time on our only source of information about the progress of the war were the Germans, since the invaders forbade anyone from owning a radio or a telephone.

We became desperate. There was a lot of confusion. Many people tried to run away, but no place was safe. Quite a number of people, especially the ones in the army or police, ran farther into Russia towards Minsk. Those were people who were cooperating with the Russians. I was told later that almost all of them were caught by the Germans and met a very bad fate. We were paralyzed because we were afraid that maybe the Russian forces would do something wrong to us. We were caught between the two giants. What would happen to us? Everybody tried to hide so as not to appear on the streets—and everyone waited to see how events would develop. A number of people were scared, expecting bad treatment from the Germans who occupied the city, and their premonition soon materialized, since a bloodbath followed very soon. The first few days were filled with panic and terror, especially when a strange noise occurred or a ring at the door.

We were afraid to leave home, but we did not witness any battles in Vilno. You could hear sporadic shots. After the first few days people were forced to go out to get some food and perhaps work. Vilno was occupied by the Germans without a battle. The Russians ran away very quickly and in their place the Germans started to organize their administration. In the street one could see German soldiers and the Lithuanian police. The latter ones, despicable men, overnight turned against yesterday's neighbors and sided with the invader.

Our situation deteriorated since Jews couldn't get jobs. I lost my old job. We had to report to the place of our previous employment and make a report about where we lived and what kind of a job we could do. Everybody from the young children to old people was obliged to register. Daily, new decrees appeared against Jews. A general horror started when street chases and house searches started, initiated by squads of the Lithuanian and German police.

Jewelry and money above an allowed minimum had to be deposited with the authorities in addition to a contribution of a definite sum, the deadline of which the Germans would not extend. There were many people stopped in the street and subjected to humiliation, especially when they couldn't understand the energetic, cleanly dressed

German soldiers, who clubbed them for this. They were forced to kneel and especially abused when they were bearded. Their beards were frequently cut off. There were some very tragic moments, and one never knew if he would come home safely. People went into hiding, but whoever didn't manage to do so, was robbed and beaten. Each courtyard had a commandant appointed by the Germans and responsible for all the residents in the house. The terror was so overwhelming, that there was no resistance, because of fear of punishment of one's family and of the whole community. The sadistic Germans held whips and clubs in their hands, supervising Jewish workers. The smallest infraction of orders, like for example a missing armband with a Star of David, brought a death sentence. The religious hatred of the Middle Ages was now transformed into the anti-humanism and 'racial' hatred of Nazism, which attached a false propaganda-label to its animalistic savagery to destroy the Jews and dominate the rest of the world. It was hard to call it psychopathological; rather, it was the incarnated evil.

Only very rarely could one meet a polite Nazi who responded to a Jewish greeting with an outstretched arm and the words "Heil Hitler."

CHAPTER TEN

ESCAPE

June and July passed in fear. The Gestapo struck heavy blows to the Jews. It was hard for me to understand how people who never knew us and had nothing in common with us could show such deep hatred. The Lithuanians and the Poles, even if they were friendly to us, stayed away and they could not be blamed. The law strictly forbade them to talk to Jews.

The anti-Jewish enactments were gradually increased and our future was ominously clouded. All Jewish organizations and institutions were closed. The invaders started to requisition Jewish furniture and houses. The expensive furniture was taken and the inexpensive destroyed. Some soldiers stole without harming Jews, while others beat them up. We had to surrender all our jewelry. In August we heard shattering news about sporadic massacres by the Germans, on some peripheral streets. Every now and then they visited some Jewish homes and took all the men with them, and nobody knew to where. Killing was done without a reason, without secrecy. Finally, they took some young men from our apartment house and the next day they returned and took some older men. None of them ever returned. We lived in a large apartment house, four or five stories, composed of maybe eighty or one hundred small apartments, in which there lived a great number of families. Such an apartment house was almost like a little village. Private homes were found only on the outskirts of the city. Very soon, the impoverished Jews started to feel miserable without furniture, without apartments and without bread. The psychological effect of the Nazi tactics desensitized us to such a degree that we could not assess the extent of the crime perpetrated on us. All this was a foreboding of worse times and one could see general expressions of doomsday.

On July 30th, the apartment house next to ours was cleared. It was a very tragic night. The Germans accused the Jews of allegedly standing on the rooftops, shooting at the German police. As a result of this, they said, one policeman had been killed and two were wounded. They said there would be a collective responsibility for this act and any future act of rebellion. This was a big lie made up and promulgated by the Germans since nobody was shooting at them. They took the entire population of the house—women, men, and children, including sick and old people—four or five hundred people all together. The children screamed. The SS men threw small babies out of the windows or, holding them by their feet, they smashed their skulls against the walls. After publicly humiliating the Jews, beating and kicking them, they drove the inhabitants forward and there was not a person left in that entire house. We never heard from them and we assumed that the Germans had executed them. The slaughter continued and thousands were not only killed on Ponary, the empty fuel pits outside Vilno, but also on the streets.

    I sometimes passed human corpses. Before they were disposed of, their gold teeth were pulled from their mouths by the Lithuanians. I could not hold back my tears, not recognizing the nature of man and the changed face of Vilno. I saw in front of me not only people with different religious and moral backgrounds, but members of different species, even though with a familiar human appearance.

What was transpiring in front of our eyes was unbelievable, like virtual reality, a nightmare. Men did not show us any compassion and God did not show us any mercy. We recognized that we had been robbed of all our legal and moral rights and that the brutal enemy had no mercy. It was just an excuse to start some "Action," and to clear the area of Jews. Two days later, on August 2nd, I remember that I was sitting in a room reading a book. The entry to this room was covered with heavy drapes. Four German soldiers, assisted by the Lithuanian police, came in and asked if there were any men. They went to every room and they looked in every wardrobe for men to take with them. They tried to get the men from every family. This time they left the women alone. Many families did not want to part with their men and there were cries and screams. We heard some shooting. After a few hours everything quieted down and we were left without the men. The soldiers who took the men away were Wehrmacht soldiers, not special SS troops. The SS had not yet entered the picture. Thereafter we had two quiet days, followed by the tragic day in which I was involved. The Germans came to our house and were taking everybody. They still were talking about the night when some of the Germans were injured, and they said that they were going to take all of us to a camp, the name of which they did not specify. They said that we were going to work since they needed workers.

People were bewildered, going here and there, crying and screaming. Nobody knew what to do. The sidewalks were crowded. This was a very grave hour. The police called on us to speed up, because they did not have much time. The ghetto edict had gone into effect. Every little apartment was cleared and the terror was increasing. There was a tumult. We did not know how to react, since nothing like this has ever happened in our lifetime. Some people, not trusting the Germans, wanted to run away. During the panic that has arisen three women and I went to hide in a public latrine that was downstairs under all the apartments. We thought that maybe they would not search the place and in this way we could save ourselves. But soon they came there also. There was a knock. When we opened the door, we saw two armed policemen. These were Lithuanians who were helping the Germans. It was a very tense moment, when the two Lithuanians took the two other girls and then one of them returned, looked at me and said, "Do you want to save yourself?" I got very scared that something awful was going to happen. I pushed him to the side, opened the door and barely made it to the outside.

I started to breathe freely when I found myself in the open. I heard some shots. When they were clearing the place, the police found some latecomers in a niche, hiding under the stairway. People tried to run away. They did not trust the Germans and their 'good will.' Finally, after the curfew, there was almost no one left.

Despite that, a few days before the Germans had taken all the men, there was one person who was detected, a rabbi who had nine small children. The Germans were very brutal and in broad daylight they gave him a murderous beating. He fell to the ground a few times and they continued kicking him in the groin and in the abdomen. This was done by the Germans and the Lithuanians There were five attackers in the group and you couldn't separate them. The rabbi's wife was sobbing violently. The little children were crying terribly and wanted to help their father. They begged, "Stop, stop, leave our father alone." It did not help. This scene is still fresh in my memory and the crying of the children still ring in my ears. This act of Nazi barbarity struck in my psyche an unforgetful imprint.

When I was in the courtyard, the Gentiles did not know who I was because I was not wearing my armband at that moment. The concierge of the house was outside with his wife and daughters. He was a Catholic. His daughters were simple uneducated girls. One of them told the police to take me also because I was Jewish. The policemen pushed me to the wooden gate, which was a small opening in the quadrangle of brick walls surrounding the complex of apartments and brought me out to the street, to join the crowd of assembled people. They were very confident that I would go there directly.

As I approached the place of assembly I saw people crying and praying. It was a very sad picture of chaos and confusion. Some of the Jews called out "God" and "Help!" Suddenly, I realized that we were not going to be sent to work. I decided to save myself. I darted away and came into the next apartment house which had been emptied a few days before. I went to the stairway and I turned my little lamb's fur vest inside out. I had a yellow Star of David on one side, on the suede side of the vest. When I changed it, it was fur only; and then the identifying sign was not visible. I heard some steps behind me and there was the concierge of the house. He came to me and looked at me. He pretended that he did not know who I was. He said, "Do you know that something very bad is happening to the Jews? In this house there are not any Jews left. Do not look for them. The only thing that awaits you is murder. Don't look for justice. Better try to save yourself."

As I went back to the street and saw the big crowd, I decided not to join them and I turned and continued on my way. But later, in fear, I wanted to go back to the group. I started to knock at the gate nervously and wanted to join the others. By that time nobody wanted to let me in. I had no choice but to look for a new place. As I was passing by, I noticed a workshop of a shoemaker. It was very low in the basement, with small windows. I talked to the shoemaker for a moment. I did not reveal who I was. He started to tell me that all the Jews who had been taken that day were going to be killed and that they were naïve to believe the Germans. They were deluding themselves, he said, thinking they were going to have a good life and work. He assured me that death was in store for the Jews. During this war anybody could be murdered, but the general knowledge is that every Jew was going to be murdered. The question was when and how much torture they would have to endure before that would happen. This was a sobering thought for me.

At this point, I decided to run farther away from that place even though that now meant risking my life. I vaguely recalled the place where Adam lived for a while. I left the boundaries of the ghetto and I came to a little apartment on the third floor on Vignu Avenue. Before the ghetto was built, my brother rented a room from a family there. This was a little away from the original ghetto sector, but not too far. I came there late at night and the people couldn't believe that I had saved myself and could still be alive. They were praying with joy. It was my impression that my benefactors understood our misfortune, because as Poles they participated in common suffering.

CHAPTER ELEVEN

THE GHETTO

The situation was deteriorating every day. More and more people were suddenly missing. The danger of being in the streets was greater than sitting at home, where the situation also seemed critical and scary with every noise and knock at the door. Later we were told that the Jews had been taken to the empty fuel pits at Ponary, outside Vilno, and executed. Men who walked in the streets were stopped and asked to present documents. Soldiers pulled the beards of the detained Jews. Nobody could understand whom and what the Nazis were searching for and how to explain their wild, savage behavior. It was difficult to endure the humiliations and violence. When would they come for me and when might I die? My brother was very fortunate because he had a document certifying that he was a practicing doctor, and they never bothered him much.

After a number of days, in the early morning, the ghetto was officially proclaimed and we were ordered to move there instantly. It meant that the entire Jewish population of the city of Vilno had to be within the ghetto borders by 11:00 o'clock, and that we were supposed to be cut off from the world from then on. All the Lithuanians knew that we would be separated from them. The Jews were told that anyone disobeying orders would be shot. Only some people saw in this the German desire to finish us off.

Everybody hurriedly left his living quarters and took with him whatever he could. Of course, it was not very much, because there were no cars or other means of transportation. There was crowding and congestion in the streets, confusion, chaos and upheaval. Some people milled aimlessly and appeared to be out of their mind. Others went by foot and some lucky ones used wheelbarrows, or transferred their belongings on handcarts. The roundup squads of policemen were roaming the city to make sure that no Jews remained in hiding there and they let us know about it. There was no secrecy.

My brother lived with a family consisting of a young couple, a dentist with his wife and a newborn baby, his sister, his brother, the brother's wife and his father and mother. We all went to the ghetto, not knowing where we were going to live, but everybody knew that we had no choice and that we had to get control of the situation. In spite of the disappointment and the dark clouds covering our skies, the hope to survive flourished. I felt sorry for my neighbors, for whom the life of a displaced person had just started, while I was already hardened by my existence as a refugee for two years. It was less embarrassing for me now to share sleeping quarters and facilities with strangers than for them. At night I heard them coughing, snoring and groaning.

The new rules affected the entire Jewish population. With the establishment of the ghetto the streets outside began to empty, while inside our small area became congested. The curfew hour was shortened. People living outside the ghetto boundary tried to transfer as many belongings as possible with them. The rest of their possessions were destined to be robbed. We, as other refugees in town, did not have these worries, since we had little.

Nobody knew how to start a new chapter in his life, after losing his old job, old business and living quarters. The trade and contact with farmers and with the Gentiles in general was officially forbidden, foreboding starvation. The enclosed ghetto was guarded by the Jewish, Lithuanian and sometimes, German policemen. Since the Middle Ages, Jews had had no similar experience and even without other German restrictions, they felt as if they had been transferred to a different planet.

A Jew had to clear the sidewalk before a German approached and, with his hat removed, keep a certain distance. Public worship was forbidden in synagogues, which were closed.

As we were coming closer, a great massacre took place outside the ghetto. The Germans, with the barrels of their machine guns raised, gathered together over three hundred people, telling them that they were bringing them to the ghetto. But the people never reached the ghetto. They were caught at the wall, which bordered the ghetto and the outside town, and shot on the spot. Thus, many families found themselves without husbands, fathers, or sisters. The family that my brother lived with lost three members of their family, and they were very depressed and heartbroken. They couldn't believe that this could happen. We heard about other abominable acts of the Nazis, who considered their behavior patriotism. They did this 'for Führer and Fatherland.' The hard ghetto life had begun.

The lodgings were very crowded. If the room was large, three, four, or even five families very often lived in one room. You couldn't bring much furniture with you, because there were no means of transporting any heavy loads. All you could bring was just a small number of belongings for everyday use. Four families lived in the room, where we established ourselves. There were only four old iron beds full of rust to serve us. The others had to sleep directly on the bare floor. Their expensive furniture was taken away by the Germans. There were even in the beginning of the ghetto people who were hungry and in a wretched state of health, but they followed the natural law of survival, the adaptation to the unusual crisis, where death waited unexpectedly on each corner patrolled by German and Lithuanian policemen. Those men, who were supposed to uphold the law, represented for us the peak of crass criminality.

We tried to establish a normal life. We tried to wash our clothes, the floors and ourselves every day, to keep a modicum of cleanliness, but pretty soon we realized that this was impossible. People brought some supplies of food to the ghetto, but within two or three days the food was gone. Later they had to rely mostly on the ration cards and the soup kitchen. The rations that we received were very small and inadequate. A few people depended on smuggling, which when discovered, was punished by death. The only hope was that you could get something from the outside of the ghetto.

Even the religious people could not follow the ritual and most of us did not know the dates of Jewish holy days.

In the beginning the Germans came into the ghetto and demanded young and strong people to work. Many registered for all possible jobs. Professional people were hiding their previous occupation and looked for any physical job, since it appeared to promise more safety. There were two different kinds of jobs, one inside the ghetto and the other outside. Usually people preferred to work outside the ghetto, because they had hopes to get some little supplement to the food that they received in the ghetto. On the other hand, there were many who were very glad to stay in the ghetto and have a small job there and just not be exposed to the outside, unfriendly world.

In the beginning I registered for a job. I went out every morning quite early and came back at night. We were constantly moving. In the beginning I felt embarrassed passing the streets for being different, which was obvious because of our yellow star that we had on. We were escorted by the German soldiers, members of the Wehrmacht to and from work. Usually the work was in plants that were working for the military. For instance, we were preparing items that could be used in the army, but not weapons. The jobs were not steady and the Germans were always moving the people from one place to another. Since there was a belief that a job for the Germans secured lives, a system of protectionism developed. You had to have money to get a job and you had to know some Germans to get somewhere.

The jobs were scarce and the population of the ghetto was diminishing rapidly. Every day some other excuse was found for making a so-called 'Action.' It meant that in the beginning they did not do it en masse, but here and there they killed four, eight, twelve, twenty victims. There was always some reason why the Germans came to the ghetto and why they took some innocent people, and, of course, there was no appeal from it. They took the Jews with them and we never heard of them.

I must admit that for a long time we did not know what they were doing with those who disappeared, since the criminal conceit of members of the most civilized and Christian nation was not recognized. We knew that the people were gone, but we didn't believe that they were being killed. The despicable acts were a reality, so horrible, that we could not believe that they were true. These unthinkable acts were not only premeditated, but a methodic introduction to a total tyrannical scourge of the entire Jewish population. This was an introduction. Later on followed the absolute evil, with robbery, burning, killings, and poisoning in the bright daylight.

My reasons in telling this story are to alert the readers to the possibility of similar events which might recur and which might affect any segment of the society. Additionally, my report is an indictment of Western civilization, which stood by silently, closing its doors to the few fortunate ones who were able to escape Hitler's bandits.

One day, in the early days of the ghetto, the military commander ordered all women and children whose husbands and fathers had been taken away, before the ghetto was established, to join them. This, of course, meant an exodus. A large segment of the ghetto population, women, parents, and children, believed the Germans. They left the ghetto and never came back. The Germans always used deception to get the people out of the ghetto without any possible resistance, but at the same time they used brutal terror.

In the meantime, life went on with never a quiet day or a quiet night even though we had become accustomed to this savagery. People, bundled up in rags, lived in constant anxiety that the Nazis could come any day and take them away. Later on there were some so-called official 'Actions.' They proclaimed that people who did not have the so-called '*schein*,' a certificate of work, were going to be moved to another place. But even those who were in possession of this certificate were warned against appearing on the street, watched by policemen. The established special policy was to issue fewer and fewer certificates of work. Our neighbor was dragged out of his room and we never heard from him again.

In order to get some hope that our existence would perhaps improve some day, we listened to the political gossip indicating that the Western Powers were mobilizing their forces to fight the German dictator. But in the meantime we were officially notified by the German propaganda that he was triumphant because his soldiers had not only conquered Western Europe, but that Nazism and Fascism would soon rule all Europe, if not the world. Only rarely were we told that the Germans had to correct their frontline for strategic reasons. Other than during those political discussions, the Germans were referred to as 'they,' to indicate their different, non-human nature. Our life seemed sadder with each of these news reports. Our new friends looked emaciated and shriveled up from hunger, but still eager to hear about an unexpected good turn of the war.

CHAPTER TWELVE

TEMPORARY SANCTUARY

I recall very well that in the beginning a hospital was a very safe place to hide and, in addition, my brother worked there. This was the so-called Jewish Hospital in Vilno. It wasn't a large institution, but before the war, it was very well-known and well-established. On the same premises, with the same number of beds, the number of patients soon multiplied. In the early phase, the Germans left the patients in peace. And the patients felt relatively safe and believed that they would not be affected. And that's why, when I did not have a job, I took shelter in the hospital. When Germans came for an inspection, I had a big scare, but they did not do us any harm. A few days later we got a warning that the Germans were planning to come again and this time remove all the people from the hospital. We were very frightened. My brother was frantic. He realized that there was almost no place to hide, especially since they were also expected to raid the homes and to take people from anywhere. There was no way for me to get a certificate of work, especially since I was all alone. I did not know anybody in the *Judenrat* (the Jewish Council, self-administration of the ghetto) because I just didn't represent much. This institution was required to deliver to the Germans people for work and for 'resettlement.' There were many people, of course, who were not refugees but people born in Vilno, so-called natives, and they were much more successful in establishing themselves.

I recall very well that I gave up all hope to survive. Knowing that the executioners were going to come, I desired some minimum security and I decided that I would remain together with my brother. I came to the hospital, where all of the doctors were already assembled, trying to hide their families there. There was a very high attic in the hospital. Since the doctors were afraid that the Germans might take us, they put up a tall ladder and they brought perhaps thirty of us up to the attic. Then they removed the ladder. When the Germans came, they shouted, looking for people all around. They were hungry for more victims. The passing hours were absolutely indescribable. I just prayed that something supernatural would happen to me and that I would not die at the hands of the Germans. I did not care at that time if I remained alive. The pressures were absolutely impossible to bear. We could hear every movement down-stairs. They spotted a ladder and we heard their climbing up, but fortunately, they changed their mind at the last moment. We could hear the shouts and the heavy boots of the Germans. We were almost certain that at any moment they would discover our hideaway. We waited for an eternity for this onslaught to pass. It was a horrible way in which this one day passed in our lives, but the following days in the ghetto also always brought some danger and some tragic event.

We were undernourished, swollen from hunger. Many of us couldn't go on. Some complained incessantly, but the majority was numb. The only thing that kept me alive was the fact that I received my moral support from my brother. He had vigor, he had hope, and he had great moral strength. He was not afraid of the Germans. He tried very much to be successful with me—to teach me to resist. Of course, he was in a better position than I was, because he always had a job and was respected. I felt, however, that the police could come any day and take me. Very often at night I hid. I did not know what to do with myself. Finally, my brother registered me as his wife, hoping that he was going to save me this way. For two weeks I enjoyed a fair amount of safety, but this couldn't last long.

Soon there came a time that the administration started to change its policy in issuing fewer certificates of work, forcing the wives of physicians to go to work. Some of the wives were successful in getting jobs with the hospital, but I couldn't get one, because I was still a stranger and I wasn't well-known to the local people. I recall that we found out that the Germans were supposed to come again. We couldn't stay in the room all the time because it was a very small place and you wanted to breathe some fresh air. We just dreamed that one day we would have a more open space. But at that time the street was very dangerous because the police could get a hold of you whenever they wanted.

The day came when we were warned that the Germans were coming. Since I did not have any '*schein*,' I was not covered again. My brother brought me to a section of the hospital, which was the wing for the mentally disturbed. He told me, "Go there. When they come, tell them that you are working as a nurse's aide." I went there and spent three days, probably the worst days in my life, living with the people that were mentally deranged, crammed in small rooms. This was not a big place and, as I recall, maybe consisted of four or five rooms occupied by perhaps over twenty patients. Some of them sang, while others banged and shrieked. It was just hell. I did not think that my nerves could take it. The cries within the compound of this little sanitarium deafened the noises from the outside. The days were not as bad as the nights. In the darkness of the night you couldn't see anything. With all the shadows, you just started to imagine that at this moment somebody would get up and hurt you. I will never forget the cacophony of noises and sounds, the breaking of dishes, spilling of soup, and the piercing whine of a young girl in her manic-depressive stage. I was almost going out of my mind and I was afraid that I was on the verge of a nervous breakdown. I was very happy when I was out of that place and I felt like a free person.

While hiding in that place, I heard the policemen who descended on the hospital like vultures. They were smashing doors and cabinets in search of hiding Jews.

As soon as I left the place I learned that during the previous two days the police had taken away my best friends, with whom I had had great spiritual ties. With the darkness of our existence, I felt very downhearted and it was hard to go on living. My brother still had a job and worked, but I was left in desperation without a job.

CHAPTER THIRTEEN

WORK OUTSIDE THE GHETTO

At some point in time, my brother decided to give up the job as a physician in the hospital and to take a job outside the ghetto. He thought that this way he would perhaps be able to get some food and improve our existence. A few times he went out to work at the airport with a large group of people, and he came back each time with a big round loaf of bread. When he came back home, looking haggard, he told me, "Marie, go quickly and sell it." He told me how much money I should ask for the loaf. I resented this very much, because I had never sold anything in my life. I felt humiliation. I did not dare offer the bread to people who could afford to pay for it while so many couldn't. There was a special place in the ghetto where people sold their wares. I paced back and forth and felt lost. I couldn't imagine myself here. It looked to me almost like begging, panhandling, but it had to be done. When I saw that some friends noticed me, I thought that this was the lowest point of my life. But nothing happened. I cried a little and then I very reluctantly sold this bread. I came home and brought the money.

This would indicate that some Jews in Poland, who were not in commerce or not in the field of selling, felt a certain humiliation from the fact that they had to sell. It's not in the Jewish nature necessarily to buy and sell. Those who are not born with this gift, particularly those from the intelligentsia, feel that there is something demeaning in it. That is why this transaction seemed to me such a big effort. I never was able to think this way. Previously, when I made money, I was just working or teaching, but I never did make money by selling. In connection with my brother's job, I recall very well, that I looked at him with pity and felt very humiliated when I saw his rugged clothes. I tried to reason that he was working at the airport and had a physical job. He used to come in with his clothes sewed up and maybe torn. How awful he looked, I thought, and how degraded he is. I just couldn't understand that he, being a doctor, could present such an appearance. But of course, from the perspective of time, I can now appreciate his courage. I believe that this is a general picture of people who are degraded in that they cannot perform the job for which they are trained. They have to do something else, physical work, when they are trained for some special professional work. We saw the unemployed intelligentsia all around us. I was afraid that Adam might be sent away and my fear grew from one hour to the next. Of no help to me were constant debates with other Jews about the worsening of our situation and of the degree of our powerlessness. At the time, Adam could not get a job as a physician in the ghetto and there were no qualifications to be met in order to become a physician in the ghetto. At that moment the ghetto was oversaturated with doctors and the population had shrunk because of the actions. So he just seized this opportunity to work as a physical worker. On the other hand, I was thinking that it was better that he was able to have contact with the outside world. During that short period when he was working outside the ghetto he had made connections with people to whom he had rendered some medical services and thus he could always bring some additional food home, supplementing the allotted very small food rations on which it was not sufficient to subsist.

This did not last long. I tried unsuccessfully to secure work for myself. For a short time I had a job. I was going outside the boundary of the ghetto and it was almost a new experience for me because, since the ghetto had been erected, I was always cut off from the outside. I felt more secure. Some young people were needed and they started to choose on a first come first serve basis. Luckily, I was chosen to be in the group of those workers. So the Germans took us out for quite a few miles. There was a large group going out every day. The soldiers always escorted us to and from work.

I cleaned and washed clothes for the soldiers and did whatever was necessary. It wasn't the Gestapo. We did domestic work in the quarters for the Wehrmacht, and we did not get anything more than our rations, just the document that we were working. This was satisfactory.

Some girls asked the Germans for food, but I never dared to ask them and I was too proud to ask them for anything. I never experienced any abuse from the Germans; however, I tried to avoid coming into close contact with them. Some girls tried to talk to them and get closer to them. They did not experience any abuse and they were not beaten, as far as I know. We were considered as if we were the property of the people who brought us to and from work and were responsible for us and watched over us.

CHAPTER FOURTEEN

MORAL AND PHYSICAL HEALTH

You could ask me about the moral life at the time before the great liquidation took place in the ghetto. Was there anything that obviously lowered moral standards? The conditions we lived in would demoralize any society. We had our underworld there, but the general population showed a great discipline and sense of communal responsibility. There was a desire to preserve Jewish life and save general cultural values.

I don't think that prostitution existed. I am not well qualified to say anything certain, because I was very far from public life and in thoughts, I concentrated on work and satisfying my hunger. However I did observe a certain loosening of morals. There was some thievery, because of hunger. The chief law was just the law of survival. I was told that some ghetto policemen were corrupt for the same reason. The conditions in which we vegetated would demoralize even angels. This was the biggest fight for preservation of life that any of us had ever fought. It often happened that a husband or a father was taken away. But even when the blow was great and while the grief lasted, the life was stronger and one had to go back to life, to normalcy. The suffering remainder of the family would start a new life, adjusting to the circumstances. Very often, if a wife, whose husband had been taken away, and who couldn't get a job, found a man in a similar family situation, she would approach him, or he would approach her, and not being a married couple they would live like one. So there were loose, not sanctioned relationships, but this could be understood under the circumstances. At the moment I couldn't believe that the people would do it so easily, because this way you created an entirely new family situation. The man went to work, brought food, and the woman considered him her husband. Religious practices and education were officially forbidden, but both secretly existed. The religious fervor that had existed before the war decreased because of the prohibition of the ceremonial ritual. The relatively unorthodox element, the teachers, who risked their lives every time they secretly taught the children, the workers and the craftsmen, were morally the healthiest element in the ghetto. In spite of a situation which has no comparison in history, Jews never lost their self-esteem and the cases of immorality were very rare.

In addition to the secret religious education there existed an approved cultural department under the auspices of the *Judenrat*. It was in charge of the schools, the theatre, choir, library and orchestra.

Being that my brother was a physician, we had connections with people who knew a little more about what was going on, I could tell that during the life in the ghetto or later, when I was in the concentration camps, I saw few people who had lost control of their mental abilities, that is to say, people who just became insane. I am not speaking about those who suddenly got depressed and committed suicide, but about people who really got insane because of the great unhappiness around them, people who would go insane after losing a member of their family. Just as I went along I saw them. I realized that the pressure of the happenings was too great for them.

These were indeed such unusual conditions, where

ethical norms accepted in a healthy society could not be applied. People changed greatly in their ways—I speak of character, of their moral standards, their ethics. In general, because we lived so close to each other, we could scrutinize our fellow men easier. The morals appeared to be looser and the values became much lower than before the war, but cases of great immorality were very rare.

In the beginning, when the people felt shocked over losses, they became insane more than they did later on and there was a number of suicides. One could buy cyanide, which afforded a quick death. They were thrown out of the balance of a normal life. This was in the first phase of the existence of the ghetto. Later on, when losses became common and also in concentration camps, when you faced death at any moment, there were fewer incidents. I know only that the hospital was overpopulated with psychopaths. These patients could not be there from before the war, because every few weeks they were taken from the hospital and liquidated and then new ones were brought in from the premises of the ghetto.

My husband tells me that during his experience in the Przemysl ghetto he saw only one man who lost his senses—when he lost his immigration documents to the United States. I saw a number of people with depression, manic-depressive characters, who, however, never became extreme in their behavior. They never became psychopaths. I believe on the basis of other reports, that in all the ghettos the changed conditions were similar and that terror, never ceasing arrests, hunger, repeated selections and psychological degradation were planned by the Nazis to break the possible resistance of the Jews.

There was a lot of stealing, something which was unheard of before the war. What do you call stealing? All the values were changed so much Strangers, with three or four families, were living in one room, which was maybe eight by ten square feet. Everybody was so touchy and sensitive, that if you lost a spoon, you thought that the guy next to you had taken it from you and you accused him. Maybe he had taken it unwillingly. If there was any stealing, it was caused by hunger, which drove even most honest people to this step. It was quite a mess. Everybody kept accusing the other person and you were just too close to the other person not to express your dislikes. On the other hand, three men were hanged and put on display in a public place for 'stealing.'

At the time, I had a job for a few weeks. Finally, however, the Germans said that they didn't need us any more, and we were confined to the ghetto. We did not have any prospect for another job for a while. In the meantime we were informed that some other people were being sent to work at our former place of employment. We suspected that probably the Germans took some money or other valuables as recompense for getting the jobs for the other group of people. Complaints and weeping did not help. To have a job was very vital. It was almost like a permit to live.

My brother lost his job, too, but he got back his old job in the hospital. I tried in vain to get a job connected with the hospital. It was almost impossible. Every day there were groups of SS coming to visit the ghetto under the pretext of inspection for cleanliness and they always managed to get some people, whom they shot in the streets or others whom they took with them. Their fate was unknown, but they never came back. We did not have any good night or any quiet day, knowing that at any time the executioners could come and take us with them.

There was no hot water and we could not get wood or coal. It was very cold and very hard to warm up anything at all. We could just wash the floors. Soap was hard to get. In the beginning we kept everything very clean and tried to do the best we could. But then as we were very often moved from our little premises to different places, we were dirty and the place became dirty. There were different people with lower hygienic standards. Finally, it turned out that we couldn't keep the place clean. With the people shifting so often, the rooms were getting filthy. Then the epidemic of typhus broke out. Lice appeared in the ghetto and everybody had them. It became awful when everybody was scratching and the infection was spreading. I did not have typhus at that time, but many other people did. The Germans did not help us to delouse ourselves. In addition to the typhus, people were swollen from hunger in the ghetto. In our hospital the nurses were helpless, because there was no DDT or anything else to delouse.

We lived in a doctors' sector, where it was relatively cleaner and we tried to keep it up as clean as we could, but the rest of the population had it much worse.

There was a shortage of bread. I did not believe, when I was told, that people with money could buy not only bread on the black market, but also baked goods. There was a general displeasure with the black marketers and street vendors, who endangered their lives, but supplied at least those who could afford it with needy items. I constantly saw people starved and swollen. I know that cases of death from hunger took place, because that's what my brother told me he saw in his practice at the hospital—he was making the rounds there several times daily. People on the street were more emaciated than swollen. Some of them looked like prehistoric creatures, especially those who for a long time did not have a job and couldn't obtain additional food. And the rations were getting smaller.

People gathered to exchange rumors, especially about politics and about the course of the war, which might still last a long time and which the Germans could still win. We thought that our situation might improve after the English air raids on German cities. But German cruelties proceeded no matter what happened on the front. We expressed commiseration to all those who became victims of hunger, death, or of epidemic diseases, and our fear of what was impending caused general depression. The individual details of the daily horrors of those days could perhaps be forgotten, but the dread of the group anxiety will stick in my mind forever, the alarming belief that we were as a group condemned to be eliminated by the Nazis after they squeezed our endurance to the extreme. The balance sheet of our situation appeared dismal.

CHAPTER FIFTEEN

LIFE IN THE GHETTO

The fight for survival was getting harder because of the everyday changes of the job situation. At a certain point I worked for two days and then, suddenly, I got the news that I had again lost my job, and with it, my vital work document. There were many so-called machinations in which people were buying the right to live, if they could buy such a certificate. The *schein* was a safe conduct pass issued to workers, which safeguarded Jews against deportation and death. The Germans were selling this certificate, using the Jews as intermediaries. I imagine that the Gestapo was instrumental in the job changes, although I am not sure of it. There were many jobs that the Gestapo men were connected with and they took our people to those jobs.

At the very beginning they asked for the fur contribution, which was the so-called *Winterhilfe* (Winter help); first they took the fur coats and then they took the good woolen sweaters. After quite some time, the needs of the front in Russia dictated that the Germans open a fur factory, Keilis, outside the ghetto. Some lucky Jews, who had the experience from before the war in manufacturing furs, found enviable employment there. Later on, when the ghetto was liquidated, the workers of this factory and of the H.K.P., which was an army vehicles park, were permitted to stay alive for a few more months, before being murdered on Ponary. Later on, from time to time, monetary contributions were imposed by the Gestapo on the Jewish population. In addition to money they took gold and silver every few weeks, especially in the beginning. Later, nobody had anything left and yet the pressures to deposit whatever valuables one still had, were very great. The contribution which the ghetto had to make was very high and everybody had the responsibility as a member of the group to contribute whatever one could. Already in the beginning of the ghetto existence we learned from the gentiles, who lived in the city, that the Jews who were previously taken had been shot to death on the Ponary hill, not far from Vilno. We did not believe them, but they gave us a very detailed description. We were horrified by the news, and we couldn't reconcile the idea that this was the truth. After a while we tried to forget. And then, in the meantime, there were other transports, other people taken from the ghetto. The Poles used to present this to us very colorfully. They said that the land around the place of execution moved, because the victims were often buried alive.

We had as the chief of the *Judenrat* at this time a man in his fifties, a man of leisure, always dressed very well, elegant. I don't know what his previous profession had been, because I was not from Vilno. But I knew that he was a rich man and that his wife was a socialite. He dressed meticulously, sporting a new pair of shoes every day. But he was more of a figurehead. The real power was in the hands of the chief of police, a big, strong man who had previously had a Zionist trade union affiliation. We had a very strong police organization in the ghetto with our own government that had jurisdiction over all internal affairs. The policemen were given rubber clubs, but used them rarely. Only some of them misbehaved, but all were disliked. Some of them were former students, merchants and professional men. There was a so-called minister of labor and a minister of finance. So it was just like a government within a government. There was a general mistrust of all those people, as they had been imposed by the Germans as their right arm.

The number of the Jewish population in the Vilno ghetto was around one hundred thousand. And the number of Jewish policemen in the ghetto was approximately two hundred. Conditions were very crowded because we only had an area of six very narrow streets in the ghetto. I remember the names of Strashun and Szawelska streets, the main street where the hospital was. They were very small, narrow, winding streets with dilapidated houses. It was very crowded. Everybody was very active in some area of cultural life, which was rich and miraculously thrived. We had a Jewish theater. We also had a group of writers and poets. Twice a week one could attend the concerts of our own symphony. There were singers and frequent lectures. I personally attended all of these quite often and started to become accustomed to the new form of life. Even a newspaper, *Geto Yediot*, circulated in secrecy.

Some of this cultural life operated under the auspices of the Germans, who encouraged us to have fun and to have our own theater. But the children were not allowed to receive any education. There was, however, the secret education of children, which was illegal. We had many teachers, very valuable people, who were undernourished just like anybody else, but felt the responsibility to teach and did it with cheerfulness. They were full of life, despite the general mood having sunk since we were forced to live in the ghetto. They succeeded in gathering the children in larger rooms and in giving them some education.

There were some Jews who were a little better off because of their connections with the Germans. They had ways to obtain additional food through smugglers. The great mass of the ghetto population was dying of hunger.

Everybody was suffering from a shortage of food and coal. I recall that the *Judenra*t established public kitchens in the ghetto. The available meal consisted of a thin soup of beans, with a small piece of bread, if you were very fortunate.

In the beginning this was a very humiliating experience for me. But I met people whose friendship I started to cherish very much. I saw them as I saw myself, declassed and in despair. Standing out from the crowd of new acquaintances was Doctor Marek Dworzecki, who kept us company in the evening and whom I was lucky to see alive many years later, during one of my visits with my husband to Israel. Even though political conversation was forbidden, we discussed the course of the war and the prospects of Jewish existence. There were some fabrications of political news and jokes reflecting the eternal Jewish humor. Even when we heard that the German Sixth Army had been defeated at Stalingrad, we did not know what to make of it. Perhaps things would get better for Jews. On the other hand, the Germans might speed up our total liquidation. There were also criticisms of the Jewish policemen and of the *Judenrat.* There was an opinion that their privileged status, which postponed the moment of their death would end, and then, they would no longer be needed to help the Germans in the delivery of other Jews. I avoided political gossip, but I participated in discussions on literature.

Despite the majority of us being hungry and worn out, we decided for self-preservation to forget the reality and to try to uplift ourselves, resuscitating the human values within us as an answer to the tormentors, who made us pariahs. We tried to attend the theater and lectures and to recite poetry. Some of us started to write short stories. I almost lost all sense of time. The life could seem, after we got used to it, great, if it were not for the other horrible aspects. Here we attended theater performances while on the same street we could hear shots and the streets suddenly became empty. The SS men were running after somebody. We never knew if they wouldn't come and get a hold of us. The conditions were extremely dangerous and many Jews succumbed from hunger, frost and disease. But the worst was the savagery of the Germans.

There was a group in the ghetto who believed in self-defense. They vowed that when the Germans would come into the ghetto and try to arrest them, they would shoot their way out. And that day came when the SS men arrived and ordered the men to go with them. When they refused, the Germans threatened to shoot them. The men got scared and threw the weapons out the window. I never found out why they were afraid to shoot their way through, as they had decided. Was it because they were afraid of their own lives, which they knew that they were going to lose anyway, or were they afraid of being responsible for the other Jews, and they did not want to cause unnecessary sacrifice in the general population? They also lacked organization. A few of them lived in one house and the others lived in the other house and they did not have good contact with each other. In other words, the underground was not well organized in Vilno. The men theorized a lot, but had an obvious lack of military skills and when it came to the deciding moment they just did not know how to act. They were young boys, who had never used weapons before and they got scared. They had just a few revolvers.

CHAPTER SIXTEEN

THE GERMAN "ACTION" (SPRING, 1942)

It was the spring. My brother had his certificate of work, '*schein*,' and we knew that the Germans would come at any time. This time they wouldn't take just a small number of people but they would make a mass "Action," according to the circulating news. The natives from Vilno decided that they couldn't have too many people working in the hospital and they told Adam that they couldn't cover him with the '*schein*.' Thus we both were left without the protective documents, knowing that this had happened at the worst time, when an action was expected. I felt very depressed. There was a nurse in the ghetto who had tragically lost her parents and had only her sister and her little brother with her. She had a '*schein*.' And she promised my brother that she would be willing to add him to her paper as her husband, which was permissible. That way he was covered.

At the last moment, when we knew that the Germans were about to come, she graciously agreed to also add me to her paper as her daughter. When the Germans came, they assembled all of us downstairs and they led us out from the hospital through the main gate to the courtyard. There, they started to select the people and whoever did not have a '*schein*' was to be sent to Ponary to be killed.

As we were presenting ourselves, people were showing their '*schein.*' I stopped suddenly. I just felt that the nurse could get in trouble for what she had done and I decided not to go. The SS man who was watching at the gate noticed me. The nurse said, "This is my daughter," but I refused to go. The SS man pushed me through the gate and hit me on the back with the butt of his gun.

When I entered this very big courtyard, there were hundreds, perhaps thousands of people, mostly old people and children, who did not have parents and did not have anybody to take care of them. All of the people without a '*schein*' were gathered there. We waited. Suddenly I faced another SS man who again started to hit me. He said, "What are you doing here? Why are you here? You can still work." I told him that I didn't have the protective paper. Blood was spilling all over me, coming from my eyes and from my nose and I had a gash on my head.

There was an old woman who tried to wash my wounds. We found a piece of cloth just to stop the bleeding. That was in the morning and the 'Action' went on for many hours. Some people were crying and shrieking, some praying. It was before nightfall when they opened the gate of the courtyard, and we spilled into the streets. They ordered us to get organized and put us in groups of eight. They promised to give us work and we marched through the streets of Vilno. On both sides there were the guards to ensure that nobody would escape. Each one of us had a little package, all the belongings that he had taken with him in case he was really going to some other place to work.

There were many SS guards and soldiers watching us with guns ready to shoot. They were very close on both sides, perhaps at every fourth row. We were marching eight people across through the snow-covered icy streets and there was no way of escaping or resisting.

It was a dark evening and, as we marched, we saw

non-Jews, who walked normally about their business. The streets were not too well lit. I estimate that it was about seven or eight o'clock in the evening. Some people from the columns tried to run away, but they were shot on the spot. We could see the corpses as we marched.

I was next to a woman, whom I knew from before as very industrious. She was with a little girl of whom she was taking care. In one hand she had a large package: bedding and big, leather officer's boots. I asked her what she was going to do with the boots. She said, "Oh, maybe at work I won't be able to earn a living, and this pair of boots could help me a lot." Finally, an idea struck me. I said to her, "Let's run. They'll kill us." She did not believe that this was possible. I said to her, "Throw your package to the ground." She refused. I said, "I am going to run away regardless of what you will do."

As scared as I was, I tore off my yellow badge, threw the package away, and slowly started to move toward the right, to be closer to the edge and within seconds I was on the sidewalk. Then I turned around and I ran.

The guards noticed that a person had moved away from the main column and they were after me. They couldn't however leave the guarding of the whole group. I mingled immediately with the non-Jewish crowd and started frantically thinking of what to do next. There was no place where I could go, because I did not have any really close friends there. I had been in Vilno for a relatively very short time and I was unfamiliar with the city. I wandered aimlessly through the streets.

Suddenly, I found myself standing in front of the beautiful church, Ostra Brama. This was a holy place, very much revered by all the Catholic Poles. As I was passing this place, I was impressed by the immense religious fervor of the people around me. I saw them crouching and kneeling in ecstasy, reciting prayers and looking straight at the beautiful image of the Virgin Mary. I couldn't pray at that moment the way they did, but all I knew was that I was just waiting for a miracle to happen. I tried to talk to my God as well as I could. I just did not believe that there was a way for me to survive, a place to go.

After perhaps twenty or twenty-five minutes standing there at the gate of Ostra Brama, I resumed my aimless walking in the city. Suddenly I met a young boy with a girl, obviously two lovers. Instinctively, I looked at them and realized that I knew and recognized them. A few months before I was taken to the ghetto, I had been going to a night school, where I took some business courses and the young man and girl were attending the same courses and on several occasions we talked at the school. I now felt closer to them and I thought I could reveal my situation to them. I approached them and asked if I could speak to them. I told them that I was absentminded, that my thoughts were now so far removed from all the people and their earthly affairs, that I was in a predicament and that I didn't have any place to go. I asked them if they would be willing to help me. I told them that I was Jewish.

After I told them about my plight, the boy said, "I am going to ask my mother. Maybe she will be willing to take you in." The girl also put in a few good words for me. She said that she always liked me very much and that she felt obligated to help me. I waited in front of their house a very short time and then they called me up. He said that his parents had agreed to take me in.

They lived on the second floor in a nice beautiful, clean apartment with wide rooms, which were very well lit. It appeared like a castle to me. When I came in, I felt like Cinderella. The people told me to wash up and pretty soon I was clean and neat, sitting at the table and eating dinner. They gave me a separate room, close to the kitchen, very clean and nice. They did not let me use any of my previous clothes. They found some little cotton dresses and underwear and they entirely changed my clothes.

In the beginning they were very touched and they were very eager to listen to my stories. They told me that they were so-called *Volksdeutsche*. They considered themselves Germans, though before the war they were Poles. As the Germans took over the territories, they found in themselves some loyalties to Germany. But they said that regardless of this, they were willing to help me. In the beginning they treated me nicely. I just had to help them around the house. The father worked at the railroad as an officer. The mother was at home keeping house. The daughter worked for the Germans as a secretary. She was perhaps not more than eighteen years old. The boy was nineteen or twenty, and there was a younger boy, age fourteen.

We had a very good relationship in the beginning and they were very moved. They did not believe that anything as horrible as this could happen. Of course, I had to be very careful and I did not want to present all the horrible truth of my side of the story and all the atrocities of the Germans, because I realized that they were *Volksdeutsche*. I did not want to alienate them too much. In the beginning, they said that they had connections with some people and that they could get me some papers—that they would be willing to provide me with a legal passport so that I could go back home to Warsaw. I was very much taken by this idea. But pretty soon the romance was to be over and they started to demand different things from me.

In the meantime, I contacted my brother through some Jewish workers who were working outside the ghetto. My brother was extremely happy when he learned that I was alive, that they had not succeeded in taking me to the place of the mass killing. As I was waiting for the papers to materialize, I was asked by this family to give them some valuables, because they were paying for my food and lodging. I gave them some knitting wool that I had, not much of it. Then my brother promised to send a few dresses and a few pieces of silver spoons for which I was waiting, from the ghetto.

Finally, the lady of the house got impatient and started to let me know that she suspected, that her husband was suspiciously good to me and that there must be something going on between us. She also started to demand from me that I go out in the street and try to go to church and that I see some other people through whose help I might be successful to find another place to live. I recall very well how desperately I felt when she sent me at six o'clock in the morning to the street, especially considering that I was afraid that someone might recognize me.

I once went to the church and then I was walked aimlessly for a few hours in the street. Finally I came back home. The woman was very happy and she thought that this would be my activity from now on every day. Her daughter started to have visitors, some German officers. While they were there, I had to hide in the house and to listen to the German songs and to the German language. I was in this house for three weeks altogether. One day I went to a movie theater. I recall that they showed a special movie for German soldiers and it was very depressing. I was glad to come home and I promised myself not to go to the movies anymore. Shortly thereafter, I made a decision. Since I just couldn't take the pressures any longer, I decided to go back to the ghetto, but my dream of returning home to Warsaw entirely disappeared. When I came to the ghetto, I joined a column of Jewish workers who worked outside. The ghetto was brewing because the killing of the Jews continued and the Germans had just taken one thousand people away to liquidate. I did not feel the strength to go on like this, but on the other hand, I did not want to be outside the ghetto. I told my brother and my friends, that whatever happened to all would also happen to me. I did not care about this life and about saving myself.

The life went on and the pressures were getting greater every day. In the meantime, I went to the library to look for a job. There was a beautiful library whose history goes back to the end of the nineteenth century. It was called *Mefis Haskala*. It was very popular with the young people. Somebody was there and made a pitch for me. They heard of my name and they said that I am from a very prominent family. I asked whether the director of the library would like to give me a job. He agreed and I started to work there. There was also another famous library, the Strashun Library. As I found out later, Germans removed books from both libraries and, supposedly, some scholars also helped them with the interpretations.

The library had one big requirement, and that was to speak Yiddish. I didn't speak it. All I could get was a manual job. The arrangement was quite good. They did not demand much from me. At least now I knew that I was working and that I had the 'paper' which entitled me to live. I worked in this library for many months. One day people came in and said that to work in the library alone wasn't safe. They said that one had to work for some German outfit.

Just about that time, they organized a factory in the ghetto, where we had to knit socks and gloves for the Germans soldiers on the eastern front because, due to the terrific cold, they were desperately in need of these things. I enrolled, and the job I was given was at night. After working in the factory during the night shift, I worked during the day in the library. For security reasons I did not want to lose this job and I also wanted to have contact with the books. It was amazing that I could combine both jobs.

The time of my work in the library passed rapidly and now I worked only in the factory, where the work was relatively light. I had a German supervisor, who showed a humane attitude, as long as we filled the quota. This was a contrast with the prevalent brutality on other outposts. We used to get washed clean socks or gloves in which we were supposed to mend the holes and to do it so exactly, that they would look just as if they were brand new. I had my own method of doing this properly so that items looked like just bought piece of gloves or socks, and they were very pleased with me. The work in the library passed rapidly and I felt a growing tension and anxiety. The situation in the ghetto was getting more desperate every day as the Germans started to feel the changing climate of the war. The propaganda of Goebbels minimized or denied all military adversities, calling them the consolidation of the German forces, or the strategic shortening of the frontline, whenever they had to retreat. In general the news, like the weather, was gloomy.

This lasted a few weeks. At the same time the competition for these jobs was getting fiercer every day, because there were a good many people laid off. Everybody knew the importance of just getting a job—and a lot of conniving went on. The job situation changed. One got a job today and then in two or three weeks was without one. The SS were coming to the ghetto more often now and committed a furious slaughter in the streets. First, they asked for the exact number of the mentally deranged. They started with the hospital population and then they asked for the old people, who were in the homes. Some influential persons tried to save their old parents. Again there was a great battle going on and lots of friction. There was a quota of human victims who were taken for execution at Ponary. The Jewish police said, "We have to deliver a set number of Jews without the possibility of arguing with the Gestapo."

The situation was deteriorating. There were instances when only children were taken. This caused big tragedies in the affected homes. The Germans, in order to avert possible physical resistance, used deception, giving assurances that the children were going to have clean, nice quarters and that they would be much better off in the new places than they were in the cramped quarters with their parents.

In the meantime, there were some changes made. The first head of the *Judenrat,* Mr. Friede, was replaced by a young, aggressive and very talented man, Mr. Jacob Gens. He was an officer in the Lithuanian army and a Jew. His wife was not Jewish. She was Roman Catholic and so was their daughter. He felt very deeply that he should help the Jews and he was with us all the way. He was a man of steel, a very terrific organizer. In the beginning, he tried to discuss the problems with the Germans, to ask them for more work passes and even to argue with them. This became particularly known after he approached them following the massacres of several thousand Jews in the autumn of 1941. He was successful on several occasions. But, as the situation deteriorated, the Gestapo demanded more and more people. Gens showed as much humanity as anybody could have, given his position in that terrible situation. But eventually he had to give in and, suspected by the Gestapo of aiding the underground, he was shot. While he was active, he was very energetic despite there being no solution. Trying to defend us he felt especially very strongly about the young people, who still were strong and healthy and who did not have the 'paper.' Whenever he saw them being taken by the police, he tried to defend them and get them away from the group that was sent to the place of execution. He falsely hoped that some Jews could be saved and remain alive. I was told that in September of 1943 he was summoned to the Gestapo and shot.

As I was working at the library, we, the entire population of the ghetto, were preparing ourselves, for the total liquidation of the ghetto. On several occasions I was taken with a group destined for liquidation, but due to the intervention of Mr. Gens, I was left in the ghetto, where the killing continued.

I decided to try my luck outside the ghetto again. When the situation and fear became almost unbearable to take, I left and started to walk out of the city. I had my yellow patch and could always put it on. I went out with a group of workers who had their jobs outside the ghetto. This was a large group and I could hide unseen. Later I took off the patch and I was mingled unnoticed with the non-Jewish people. I went to visit with some people who lived maybe thirty or forty kilometers away from the ghetto on the property of Count Radzivil, who had left Poland before September, 1939. The property was administered by his manager, who was a Lithuanian. This man, with his wife and the wife's sister, took me in. They were generous and nice to me and treated me well. They knew my brother very well because, as a physician, he had taken care of them before. They felt obligated. As a matter of fact, they praised him so much that I almost felt embarrassed. They told me, "Oh, we feel just like he is our brother." This was very flattering.

Life on this very large estate was pleasant. It was a beautiful place in the clearing, surrounded by the forest. It was built in the French style with beautiful columns in the front and with big stately oaks. The house had a pretty design. I stayed with them three and one-half days, but I finally concluded that this was too sweet a life for me. I could not adjust to this living. I went back to the ghetto.

I learned that our apartment in Warsaw, which we had just gotten in January 1939, was taken over by the Germans, who were stationed there. They converted it to a small first aid station.

A few times we knew in advance that the Germans were coming into the ghetto, because some windows of the ghetto were facing the free world; thus, we could spot them. When this happened, we hid in the bunker. It was deep, perhaps twelve or sixteen feet in the ground and perhaps six to eight feet wide. We always took a little food with us when we stayed there. Everybody prepared himself for the worst. We knew that sooner or later we would be taken.

Some people had hiding places high in the attics. I remember this very well. One time the SS men took three to four thousand people. One time, there were many families hidden in the attic, where I was. We could hear every step of the Germans and their voices. They were pounding at every door and kitchen cabinet. We stayed in the attic a day and a night. Some of the bunkers were discovered by the SS and by the Lithuanian police and the people were drawn out of them. We were lucky not to be discovered. Finally when the orgy of the 'Action' was over, when the shots and the noise quieted down, we came out and went back to our rooms. The evacuation of the Jews from the ghetto was unbelievable. We learned that many people whom we knew had been taken. I was told by an agitated friend what was happening in the streets, that when somebody tried to address a German, he was kicked and told to keep moving. The population of the ghetto was dwindling. On the deserted street I saw the scattered belongings of the deported. We still could not believe that this was reality.

There were in the ghetto some underground activities, from which eventually emerged the United Partisan Organization, F.P.O. I am not familiar with the details, but Adam started to plan self-defense at the same time and the head of the resistance group, Yitzhak Wittenberg, got in touch with him. The partisan organization was interested in Adam, because he was a physician with past military training.

Wittenberg sent a message to Adam, inquiring whether they could meet in a secret place to discuss urgent business. When they met, he told my brother that he had decided on an armed revolt within the ghetto, asking Adam for cooperation. The situation had not yet matured for an immediate decision, said Wittenberg. Adam, faced with the practical consideration of defense of the ghetto, immediately assessed the plan as futile. The situation was hopeless. The young people did not have enough weapons and ammunition to defend themselves, they lacked military preparation and their plan to fight inside the ghetto was destined to fail. The weapons, which had been smuggled into the ghetto, were an insignificant deterrent to the heavy armor of the Germans. Adam felt that the Jews, living frequently in the past as storekeepers, artisans and professional people without a military tradition, could defend themselves only under cover of the forest, where they could hope for cooperation with Polish or Russian partisans. Adam suggested that his plan was to fight outside the ghetto, that it was worth the risk to leave the ghetto and to explore contact with the partisans. There were other members of the resistance who shared Adam's view that the only chance for success was to run into the forest, but Adam did not have any connections with them. They eventually went to the forest, but most of them were wiped out in their fight with the Germans. Wittenberg was eventually arrested in July 1943 and then rescued by the Jewish partisans while being led from the Ghetto to Gestapo headquarters. He had been betrayed by a Polish communist who was tortured by the Gestapo. There were two versions describing his death: one was that he had killed himself; the other was that he had been murdered by the Gestapo. After his death, Vilno, once a great center of Jewish culture known as the Jerusalem of Lithuania, Yerushalayim de Lita, was about to cease its existence. Two months later, in September, the ghetto was liquidated. When we started to feel that the last days of the ghetto were approaching, my brother decided that there was not a moment to lose and that the decision had to be made immediately. He was able to leave the ghetto and to be transferred to a small place, Zezmarai. It was a Lithuanian town with a large camp of T.O.D.T. This was a German engineering organization. There were over one thousand people working there. At a certain point the Germans brought many people from the surrounding towns of Baranovicze, Swieciany, Grodno, Lida, and Vileyka into the Vilno ghetto. After taking away their businesses, they robbed them of all their possessions and did not even leave them with a crust of bread. They came on foot, some with knapsacks on their backs. In the camp of T.O.D.T. where my brother got work, there were still some people from those little towns. Some of them succeeded in bringing their parents and children there. Adam, with another doctor, was taking care of those people. There was nothing that I could do. We had a standing agreement that whenever the Germans would decide to liquidate the ghetto, he would come to the ghetto to save me. And whenever they would liquidate his camp he would be able to come back to the ghetto.

We lived under great pressure. Because of collective responsibility, we were spied upon by our own people. As it was in the ghetto, there was a leader in charge and all the people watched each other. Wherever you went there were some eager eyes following, and also eager steps. There were a few 'Actions' during which even people with the best jobs and qualifications were taken away. There was a group of over one thousand who left the ghetto each day to work outside in the town of Porubanek. We all felt that theirs was a sure job, that they were secure. But once they took them to the job and they never returned. We were constantly afraid of even more brutal conditions awaiting us when we would be deported. We thought the conditions could even be worse than inside the ghetto, but we couldn't imagine a total extermination. The Germans tried to break our spirit to resist by their deceit, and terror.

CHAPTER SEVENTEEN

FROM GHETTO TO CAMPS

One day, in the early part of 1943, a list of new victims was circulated in Vilno. I was told that I was on this list because I didn't have anybody to cover me. I felt hopeless and I tried to contact my brother. On that day, in the morning, the entire ghetto was surrounded by big German SS trucks and all of the exits were well guarded. They came into the ghetto with the list of the people whom they were going to take. It was Friday, a day of the week chosen most commonly by the German for unknown reasons, for their *Actions*. I knew that my last moment had come. Then, suddenly, I saw my brother coming with the Germans from his outfit, the friendly Todt people, whom he was secretly treating. They demanded that I go with them. Fortunately enough, they arrived before the SS men. I left with them, and with great pomp I left the ghetto and came to the camp, Vievis.

I stayed in Vievis about a month and afterwards I was transferred to Milejgany. Both were little places in the countryside of Lithuania. From there we went to Zezmarai. Zezmarai was a much larger camp. There was a time that we had it fairly quiet. Every morning we went to work and after sundown we came home.

When I came to that camp, the life was entirely different than before. There were still some families living together from the small towns around Vilno. My brother soon assumed the leadership in this camp. He debated with me going to the forest for a long time and finally asked me: "We have to get ready for any eventuality. We will have to go to the forest. Will you go with me or not?" I thought for a while, and in fear for life in the forest, I finally replied: "No." In his determination he fiercely concluded: "You will regret that."

The Jews were preparing themselves to resist and he was the leader of the resistance group. At the same time he was on very good terms with the Germans and he even took care of them on several occasions, which was against the law, but there was no social contact with them and he had no special privileges. They were much more approachable than the SS men, but they had their own lives outside the compound. As I recall, the camp was not surrounded by a fence. So it looked like just a labor camp.

In the morning, when we left for work, we were escorted by a German soldier with his drawn rifle. At the very end of the working column there was another German and there were two or four in between. So we were not guarded too well. We were working in the country, some close to the river, some in the woods and others in the fields. We helped with the harvest. Later, when we worked in the woods, we were cutting down the trees, carrying them and putting them in one place. We had to split them into smaller pieces.

The peasants were very friendly. They were always willing to give us some food. We used to come home and after we got our rations we were tired and went right to sleep. The quarters were very inadequate.

One day in the heat of the summer the SS men came with their *Obersturmführer*. Their trucks were waiting outside. They surrounded the camp entirely. The officers came into the camp and asked for some young, strong men whom they needed for work. A big panic and consternation started. The SS took twenty men, who were the cream of the crop in the camp, with them. They promised to let us know when the job would be done and when the men could come back, but they never came back.

Some new arrivals brought us news that the Vilno ghetto had officially liquidated by the oppressors on September 1, followed by skirmishes with the Germans and the Jewish partisans.

At the end of October 1943, the SS men again came in great numbers. Two days prior to this visit the Jewish administration of the camp was preparing some lists and we knew that something was brewing, but we were not sure what it was. This time the Germans were asking that the children be delivered. This was the most gruesome picture of all because all the mothers and fathers were shocked and tried to hide the children in boxes and behind clothes. The soldiers started a hunt all over the camp, but we were still successful in hiding close to fifty children.

One day in December 1943 the Gestapo came with the SS and brought an ugly surprise. They demanded people. They saw some children whom they decided to take. I recall three officers together. One of them, in his forties, well-dressed and handsome, saw a child and said, "Why are you crying, sweet girl?" And she said, "I am crying because my mother left me." Actually, her mother hadn't left her, but she panicked and ran away somewhere in the camp. The SS men and their officers started to discuss the matter—how "mean" the mother was that she had left her child alone. One of them said, "Come with us. We are going to take good care of you." They took the child.

Then, later, they decided to clear the camp entirely of the children. They took some older people, the children, and some people who were unable to work. This time the mothers decided to put up a battle and not to give up the children easily. This was a terrible fight. The women fought only with their fists and they wanted to go with the children. But the SS men did not permit this. They assessed the mothers and said, "Oh, you can still work. You leave the child alone. The child will be better off without you." The mothers screamed, cried, and begged the SS men to take them with the children, because the children couldn't manage without their parents, but to no avail. They were brutally pushed and the children were taken. Nothing could be imagined which was more shattering and horrifying than the cry of the mothers. As during each of the previous "Actions" we heard shots. Several people were killed.

Beginning with this day the resistance group decided to find a solution. They thought that there must be a way to leave the camp and to fight, to try to get some freedom. Peasants told us that the partisans in the forest were getting ready to start their sabotage activity, but they wanted the young, strong men, preferably with a military background, to join them. The peasants were specially sent by the partisans and some people made contacts with them and decided to join them. There was a meeting during which my brother told the young resistance group that next time they were not going to let the Germans take anybody. They thought that if they were able to meet the people from the partisan group in the forest, maybe something could be arranged that would benefit the entire camp population. There were some objections to joining the guerrilla forces. As the Germans came more often to take people, the population of the camp dwindled and not too many strong and able-bodied people were left.

After this last 'Action,' my brother was really depressed. The weather did not help. A storm raged. My brother made contact with the partisans and got a gun. On several occasions he asked me to go with him to join the guerrilla forces, but I objected, saying that I was too weak and didn't feel that I was able to do it. The picture of the children brutally taken away from their mothers, and their mothers beaten and even shot, affected me very much and I started to change my mind about somehow leaving the camp. I decided to stay where I was, dogged by the thought that Adam would eventually leave for the forest and I would remain alone.

An alarming incident had occurred, which raised the fear of German retribution. My brother and I had planned to leave the camp on a Wednesday when it was market day and some people with the carriage were supposed to come pick us up. It was quite a long way to our destination. Without telling me, he left to reconnoiter the area, before taking me to the forest. As usual, I went to work on Tuesday morning—this was the end of March 1944—and my brother, being a doctor, worked in the camp. At work, I suddenly got a very bad premonition: perhaps this morning was the last time that I would see Adam. In the evening when we started to walk home I felt like something awful was going to happen. When I came home there was a big commotion in the camp. Adam slipped unnoticed through the German and Lithuanian lines, but I did not know anything—where he was going and what he was going to do. And the Jewish leader came to me and started to ask, "Where did he go? What happened?" I was not able to furnish them any answers, because I really did not know. I realized that my brother finally had made a decision because he could not take it any longer and he did not feel that it was feasible to stay in the camp. He was on very good terms with the Germans that were running our camp. The next day, in the morning, everybody went to work and we anticipated bad news. The alarming incident of Adam's flight raised a general fear of German retribution. Three other young men also decided to leave the camp. On the evening of the next day, the German leadership of the camp asked me if I knew where my brother had gone, and they started to interrogate me. I was not of much help. I still had some flickering hope. Finally, the Todt people asked me, if I knew that my brother had been intercepted. I did not know anything and the news hit me like a bolt from the blue sky. They tried to use very strong language with me and were almost brutal.

Then the Jewish leaders came to me unexpectedly and told me the whole story. I had no particular reason to distrust their words. They said that my brother had left the camp and took off his yellow star, walking freely. He went quite far, to his Lithuanian friends at the palace of Prince Radziwill. When I heard this I was almost relieved, because I believed that nothing bad could happen. One thing I was sure about—he was very tall and blond and blue-eyed—and that was that nobody would recognize him as a Jew. He came to the people who had told me before how very much they liked Adam and that they considered him as their own brother. The woman, however, seemed not to recognize him, or pretended she did not. He started to talk to her and he asked about her husband. She told him to wait a minute, that she would bring her husband. She left and brought the German police. I understood that the door was closed and my brother was in real danger. He was caught outside the ghetto with a gun. The Germans arrested him and interrogated him before the execution. First the Jews and then the officers who were Todt people, gave me those details about Adam and left. They couldn't tell me anything more and they were very sorry. There was a cold howling wind and I stood there and did not dare to cry. I found myself in boundless misery after the loss of the only support that I had in life.

They came back to me late at night and said, "It's too late. Adam was left alone in his cell before the interrogation and committed suicide. He hung himself on his belt from his slacks rather than reveal the identity of his comrades to his torturers." This happened in the Gestapo jail on April 1, 1944. With tears in my eyes, I was shocked by the news. That's how I lost my brother. I was grief stricken and scared of being caught and executed for being his sister. I spent an exhausting night not being able to close my eyes. I tried to repress the reappearing image of his hanging body and I was plagued by my decision not to go with Adam when he asked me to, and with this thought, I constantly reproached myself for a long time. Perhaps, if I had decided to go with him, he would have planned differently and survived.

The Todt people said, after Adam's death, "We decided to close the camp because we didn't see it feasible to work with you." There prevailed in the camp an atmosphere of great tension and anxiety.

A decree was announced to liquidate the camp and the SS people came and did just that. There was a panic of deportation. We were standing in formations. They divided us into separate groups: the people who still were able to work, to the right; and the people like the parents, the weak, the sick, and the children (the few that were still left) went to the left. Those chosen during the segregation to be on the left were killed. I was fortunate to go to the right. The Germans brought us to freight cars, which took us on a journey to an unknown destination. We arrived at Kaiservald, in Estland, in Estonia, where we worked mostly in the forests cutting wood and carrying it, collecting it in one place and then chopping it into smaller pieces. Soup and a small piece of bread once a day had to carry us till the next day. We were brought to work by the SS men with their

Finally, we were taken to Panevezys Flugplatz. We came back to Lithuania, rifles always ready to shoot. Here there were very many people. This probably was previously a military camp, now surrounded by a barbed wire fence. We were building trenches. From there we were sent to Siaulai, also in Lithuania. Then we went to the Gefangenlager in Kaunas-Kovno, Lithuania. We were just slaves. Epidemics started—dysentery and typhoid fever. We had Jewish nurses, although at this stage of the game, we did not have any Jewish doctors.

After our work was finished in July of 1944, suddenly the SS men and great numbers of Gestapo men surrounded the camp and told us, after ordering us to bring money and all our valuables, to stand in line. They announced that they would take us on a new job. We expected the worst, because of the enormous numbers of German SS men on the ground and many on the trucks. But still nobody thought of running away. It was impossible because we were entirely surrounded. The Germans told us that any attempt to escape or hide would be punished by death. We were in a place where we did not have any outside friends and at this time nobody probably would have let us in.

It was warm and the weather was splendid. We were herded into the waiting train amid the wild yelling and cursing of the Germans, who kicked and beat all those who were moving too slow. Breathless and fighting for air, we occupied our standing places pressing against those who were around us. I was exhausted and used my last reserves to keep myself on my legs. The train was surrounded by German and Lithuanian police.

It was an enormously long freight train with small boxcars. There were no windows. We felt like helpless cattle destined for the slaughterhouse riding in sealed freight cars. Each of the freight cars was heavily guarded. Life on the train was hopeless, throwing us into almost total darkness. We were not allowed to go out and the space was crammed. There was not a breath of fresh air and the temperature rose unbearably. In Lithuania, before leaving, we were given our ration. There was a general thirst. People were fainting and begging for water, but there was no response from the Germans. Somebody suggested that this was perhaps how the Gestapo wanted to exterminate us. We were on this deportation train for more than two days, which seemed to be the limit of human endurance. We had one dishpan and a pail on the car and that is how we were supposed to take care of our needs. We were embarrassed and mortified, but what could we do? The smell was nauseating. People felt very weak and were getting sicker all the time. One woman died. Late at night we were transferred from this train to a different one.

I don't remember where this transfer took place. We were going through East Prussia, part of Germany. We were transferred into a very small train and the railroad tracks were very narrow. It just looked like a terrible nightmare. All the time this was happening, I thought of Dante's *Inferno*. I couldn't perceive that this was real, that this most progressive and intelligent society as the Germans were, was able to treat people in such a bestial way. The rest of mankind stood by, knowing full well what was happening and did not react, or worse, was tacitly satisfied that Hitler had done the dirty job of ridding Europe of Jews. If we were condemned to be killed, why expose us to such suffering before that? But in spite of hunger, beatings, and psychological degradation, we, the victims, still wanted to preserve our naked life in this hell. The Germans destroyed our scale of human values and human dignity. While all this was going on, we could not even recollect a normal lifestyle, home, family and friends. The common hell that we lived in brought us together, whatever our past social standing and education was: we were equally exposed to the plunder and to the brutality of those, who called their victims sub-humans and constantly pointed their guns at us.

I did not believe that I was a part of this tragic story. In this little train the cars were open, just like trucks—so that we were able to look around, but everything was pitch black. Nobody tried to jump because nobody was physically strong enough to do this and no one was emotionally ready to make such a decision. The situation grew graver every minute. We were just waiting for the worst to happen. We did not know anything about what was going on with the war. We did not know that the course of the war had changed so greatly. Actually, that was the time when our greatest misery just started.

Finally, our train reached its destination and we saw some mysterious lights and we came to the camp, Stutthof, men and women of all ages. This camp was under the leadership of the Gestapo and controlled by the SS guards. The political prisoners were under the supervision of the Gestapo, but we were watched by the SS and their vicious dogs.

The land was flat and wet. The entire camp was fenced with two rows of electrified barbed wire with observation towers and searchlights. After a short time during which we remained motionless, we were ordered to deposit all our personal belongings in baskets and we were taken from the train and dispatched to our huts. We were taken from the train and marched to our barracks, flanked by guards, in darkness, which had set in a long time ago. We were directed towards the so called *Judenlager*, separated from the rest of the camp.

When we entered the camp there was real bedlam. Everybody was running to and fro. They first put us into large, empty rooms, women separately and men separately. This appeared to us as if it were a strip of land with some walls around it and a roof. We expected to be assigned to different quarters and we knew that we were going to be searched. They told us that we were going to take a bath because we were stripped of all our clothing. All our belongings were taken away. There was panic on every face. Some people still had wedding rings or earrings and they tried to dig a little hole and hide their items in the ground with the hope that they would come later and recover them. The horrible life in the ghetto, as stunning as it was, paled in comparison with the terrible events of the coming time. I trembled all over. My recollection of life in the ghetto is more accurate than my recollection of life in the camps; perhaps that is because I tried to suppress the memory of the hell seen in the camps with the daily murder and corpses loaded on lorries.

There was an immediate roll call with counting and beating. The men were separated from the women. We were told that since it was late, we would have to stay in this temporary shelter and the next day we would go to the bath and to our little quarters. Everybody was tired and cold but managed to sleep through the night. I could barely turn from side to side, because of the pressing body of my neighbor. Early in the morning we were taken away in groups of twenty. We went through a screening and then to the bath, and afterwards, we were handed clothes from a big pile that was in the open. We didn't know whose clothes they were. Nobody was getting the clothes that fit him or her.

Pretty soon we were supposed to be examined by a doctor. We were brought to a so-called hospital and there they checked our health. All the time we were assisted by the SS men and closely guarded and watched. In the hospital two doctors and a few nurses checked us. The nurses were supposed to help us and they tried hard to gain our confidence, hoping to get some valuables in return. The examination was a real mockery. We stood entirely naked waiting for our turn. First our hair was checked and then our eyes and mouths. There was a long search in the mouth for anything hidden there and anybody who had any gold teeth was marked on the chart. In the hair they were also looking for items that we might have hidden. Then there was a very thorough vaginal examination whose need we couldn't understand.

After this humiliation we were sent to the little rooms, which were like those in a military camp. Everybody had his place, where he was assigned. I was put on the far west of the camp, where I found myself with some three hundred other girls. There were two rows of iron beds, which were doubly stacked and very uncomfortable. There was a little straw that we had to bring from the outside and stuff them in sacks. In some places the girls did not have enough room so that they had to sleep together, two or three in a bed. The little straw in the sack afforded little protection against the frost. We therefore huddled as close to one another as we could in the hut and, if possible, outside during the *Appell*.

Our real misery was to begin at that time. Some women despaired that they had been taken away from their families. It meant that from now on they would have to be alone, without husbands or children. In the evening we were given a bread ration which was to be sufficient for the whole day, and then a watery turnip soup. Usually there was a woman who was responsible for this part of the camp, and only through her could we discuss any matters concerning our camp and our life there. There were special rooms for the foremen. They took care of dividing the bread and margarine and made sure that everyone got the soup and that the division was proper. They were dressed like the other inmates in striped uniforms. At night, when we went with our little bowl to get the soup, bedlam ensued once again. Everybody looked at the other person's bowl. They all felt as if they had been cheated and had not received enough. The turnip soup was very thin and we were constantly hungry. All day we had to work under the eyes of our supervisor in a weapons factory. Exhausted, we looked forward to the silence and darkness of the night.

The next day we were introduced to brutality and violence and to the man who came to be very much connected with us. His name was Maximilian, Max for short, and he was the man who decided about our life or death (*dominus vitae necisque*). Later we learned that he had been incarcerated in this concentration camp for a felony crime. He was a tall, dark man and we were told that he was of Polish extraction. He wore a green triangle on his uniform, indicating that he was a criminal. This did not help us much because he was as rude and mean to us as he could be. There is no way to describe atrocities practiced by him on individual women. Whenever he found it necessary to interact with us, he caused a lot of suffering and always exposed us to his vicious cruel acts, as if he might get some delight in torture. He told us to run and to exercise. In German he ordered: *Hinlegen*—lie down, *Auf*—get up, which we followed as many times as he decided. Sometimes, it seemed that this would never end. It was obvious that he wanted to finish us off. When he picked only one or two victims, the rest of us were left in peace. He picked a girl and tossed her down several times, climbing up on her torso. Those occasions were rare. While beating people, his face became red and then, when he looked at us, he seemed to enjoy creating a fright with his appearance, also seeming to enjoy the swollen faces and black eyes that were the result of his beatings. While beating a woman, in his sadistic frenzy, he would verbally abuse his victim, calling her *"Du judischer Schweinerhund!"*—you Jewish swine dog Those who passed out were carried back to the room by the others. During one of those exercises we lost a young woman. Her body was brought to the roll call, when the living and the dead were counted. The daily roll call, known as the *Appell,* occurred in the morning, and after work, in the evening. The SS-men checked the numbers of the inmates and also used this occasion as a form of public punishment, letting us stand in the freezing wind, sometimes for hours. We stood there shaking, wearing only our striped uniforms. Whenever our tormentor entered the rooms, he always looked for some scapegoats whom he whipped. The nights were very cold. Very often, we were awakened by him at night with the whistle and the call, "*Aufstehen*," get up. We could not understand this cruelty and why people behaved as they did. Everybody had to get dressed quickly and the quarters were checked for those who were slow. As we stood outside, shivering and trembling, Max watched us and always managed to humiliate and abuse us, and as often as he could, to beat us up. There were a number of girls who wound up in the hospital as a result of his treatment. We were told later that the girls who were in charge of us, also had a criminal past, and some of them were prostitutes before their incarceration.

    I felt overwhelmed by the evil and insanity, which were on one side of the scale, while intelligence, brotherhood and progress were on the other. Our lives and indeed, in a broader sense, world peace, hung on this balance. I did not dare think about the future, because I felt that the present was as hellish as life could be. If we should perish, the devils around us would not be satisfied with this solitary act, but they would continue killing and destroying others and blaming their victims. This was no mystery.

    Germans used us to build a road. We were issued heavy hammers and instructions how to cut the stones and to carry them to the assigned place. A woman was slapped in the face for not properly holding the hammer. Thank God for fresh air! But the hard work in the heat of the day, which lasted till dark, caused me to have a shoulder ache. We developed muscle pain, but were afraid to complain. Hungry and exhausted, we marched back to our quarters, supporting those who were fainting. We were too exhausted to talk. Soon after we arrived at our destination, we were called to the *Appell,* during which the number of inmates was verified. If we were lucky, it lasted a short time. Afterwards the soup was distributed. We didn't have enough water to wash our bodies. We fell dirty on the straw sacks of our bunks and fell asleep to the accompaniment of barking dogs from far away. The early morning would see us again, ready for the *Appell*, the head count, trying to avoid beatings and humiliations. We were so used to being whipped that we considered it an abnormal day when nobody got whipped. Then we walked five abreast back to work.

I recall very vividly, how, in the beginning, some of the girls would suddenly notice from far away, in the men's part of the camp, a member of their families, a brother, father, or a husband. They rushed to the fence to exchange a few words, not knowing that the fence was charged with high-tension electricity. They were instantly electrocuted and in a flash their body was turned into a lump of skin and bones. One small shriek and one of our women was gone. We saw it and couldn't help.

We also became accustomed to the executions of all these innocent people, which became part of our daily experience

New transports of Jews continuously arrived at our camp. We saw the Germans beating them with rifle butts and with their fists. We rarely heard a scream or a complaint. Occasionally, the body of a victim who had been shot was carried away from the crowd. The well-clad newcomers soon looked just like us, as they were dressed in their camp uniforms. The foodstuff in their luggage, the tea and coffee, were confiscated.

In the latter part of July following an announcement of the arrival of a new contingent of inmates, we received a big transport of Hungarian Jews. This was quite late in the war and they would be exposed to this horrible experience for the first time. They were bewildered and couldn't find themselves. It was just like taking somebody from a warm bed and bringing them to the wilderness of the camp. They felt lost and had no confidence. They couldn't understand the cruel treatment to which they were exposed and why they were to go to bed hungry and be beaten. I very often saw how they looked at us after they ate their portion and they begged us to give them more, not realizing that maybe we were suffering more than they, because we had behind us long years of tragedy and hunger. We were supposed to bring them hope. On several occasions I gave them some of my soup. Later, others laughed at me, saying that the Hungarian girls were getting as much as I. But I very much sympathized with them because I saw that they were not yet adjusted and they needed a little tender care. Beaten, shaved, unwashed and hungry they soon lost all their feminine charm and their sudden troubles dulled all human desires other than hunger. Eventually they started to huddle close to us. We were told pretty soon that we were going to be sent to another camp. In our camp there were many other nationalities.

Autumn began with cloudy days and the occasional rain. We were completely cut off from the world. Sometimes, the only sound we heard was the barking of a distant dog. This did not change the daily routine of our slave labor. Now, in addition to intestinal disorders, people started to get respiratory tract infections. Many were coughing and spitting all through the night. On top of everything, lice appeared. It was a fight for every hour and like the outdoors, where the intermittent rain changed into a downpour, the general mood of the people was depressed. Some girls developed pneumonia for which they were 'treated' in the camp infirmary. This was a place that everybody tried to avoid, since the patients were usually executed. The number of dead women grew daily. Daily, we faced mud, torture and death.

One of my good friends in this camp had the wife of a physician before the war. She was a very fine woman, who suffered greatly because the ration did not match her constant hunger and there was no way to satisfy her. She walked as if she were in a daze and finally decided to do something radical. In her friendship she patted me on the head and shared with me her pearls of wisdom, saying that we had to find a way to live even with those devils around us. She approached a German and asked him for a domestic job. Fortunately, he let her clean up his quarters. This was the *Obersturmführer*. Every evening, when she came back from work to our room, she brought some bread or soup, which she shared with me, a wonderful thing to do under our circumstances. She did this after we had been friends for some time. She had this job for a few weeks. The additional food took care of the terrible hunger pangs that we suffered and I shared it with some of my other friends.

There was one other thing that complicated the life of my benefactor. Pretty soon she started to crave for cigarettes, since she was addicted to tobacco. There were some other girls who were also addicted and began to feel very badly without cigarettes. I never smoked and I couldn't understand this addiction. It was, of course, impossible to get any cigarettes.

There was a man, a Pole, who worked in our camp checking the electricity. He was the only contact with the outside. When I struck up a conversation with him, he told me that the war was going much better and that pretty soon we would be free. He said: 'Chin up' with a mysterious smile. He was perhaps not a philo-Semite, but a decent human being. He said that the Germans were getting beaten on all fronts and that there was a *putsch* in Germany and some generals had tried to assassinate Hitler, although unsuccessfully. We hear from him about the Jewish uprising in the Warsaw ghetto and about the Russian offensive. He used to come a few times a week and this was the only contact that we had with the outside world. He showed warm feelings toward us and always promised that the next time he would bring us some better news. But in the meantime we had to go through the nightmarish state at the concentration camp with constant beatings, ill treatment and torture. Some girls thought that the more the

Germans bled on the front, the quicker they would proceed with the extermination of the remnant of the Jews.

And I recall when they gave me my clothes; they were in the form of an oversized man's coat. When I told them that I didn't need a man's coat, they told me to shut up and to be glad that I got something. We were also handed the striped shirt and underwear that, from that time on, would be our official clothing. Some girls were lucky and managed to get dresses or even sweaters. I received a very fancy batiste dress that tore immediately. I tried to get another dress, but it was impossible. Nobody listened to me and as time went on, I froze more and more. I had the same bad luck with the shoes. Some girls managed to get very good, sturdy shoes, but I got a pair of very miserable looking shoes, which were stolen after the first week in the camp. I was left without shoes. At night, when I had to go outdoors to the '*Appell*,' to which all the girls from our little block had to appear promptly, I shivered tremendously. My barefoot legs ached in the cold. Then Max told us to run and, with his whip, he tried to make us run quicker.

Later, I heard that the Germans had put a group of inmates from Stutthof on a ship on the Baltic Sea and then they had set the ship on fire. The ship blazed for over two days and almost all the inmates perished.

They segregated us. Again, the Germans examined us and they sent the people that they felt were physically fit and healthy to work in Stutthof's sub-camp, Steinort, which was under the auspices of the main camp in Stutthof. The new camp was surrounded with an electrified barbed wire fence with observations towers manned by a small number of SS men, the embodiment of sadism. When they caught a Jew, they beat him mercilessly or gave him a number of lashes with the whip, of course without reason. There was a constant sound of yelling and screaming and one could hear the cracking of the whips on the backs of the poor victims. Sometimes, the beating was so savage that the Jew, if he or she were left alive, looked like a bloody pulp. We learned to avoid contact with any SS man. The silent crowd, surrounded by *kapos* and SS-men, marched in complete darkness and entered the wooden barracks in an atmosphere of deep anxiety. Even though it was located in Poland, I had not heard about the place before the war. In the beginning, we did not know where we were. We found out later. We had to follow orders about how to live and what to do, and we were given strict punishment for any deviation.

The downpour and bitter cold continued, but it made no difference in our work and in the way we were treated by the Germans. We were working in the mud, sometimes wading in puddles of the flat land and standing ankle-deep in water. I dreamed about a roof over my head or at least a coat. My wet rags soaked with water stuck to my body and slowed my movement. I slid down numerous times and was constantly freezing.

It finally started to snow. The days got shorter and since we worked only during the daylight, we got a few more hours to rest.

My bed of boards was on the lowest of three levels and any dust from the straw sacks, caused by the movement of my neighbors who slept on the upper layers, fell on me. Nobody spoke. Exhausted, we fell almost immediately to sleep.

From time to time we were visited by the *blockalteste*, a woman in charge of our block, who wore a black triangle on her uniform, indicating that she was a prostitute. She was feared because of her cruelty. Rumor had it that women like this one did not serve only the German Fuehrer, but that the SS men also used them for their gratification.

As we stood in the frost during the *Appell*, we saw exhaled vapor coming out of our mouths and we felt the inhaled stream of air almost freezing in our noses, while the

SS-men on the watchtowers were dressed in warm furs and boots. The SS men around us were well fed and they moved with their whips in their hands, always ready to strike, occasionally shouting and lashing to the right and to the left, without apparent reason. In our rags, we looked at their leather coats and clean-shaven faces as creatures from another planet. Our group was getting smaller, because of the number of sick girls that were removed to the 'hospital'. The hopelessness of our existence was indescribable. We didn't dare dream about freedom, because it was enough to worry about surviving another day. We exchanged very few words with each other, saving our energy for talking. One could hear only the constant sounds of coughing and moaning.

My teeth chattered and my body shook from cold. I cried from weakness and dried my tears with the sleeve of the dirty, torn striped dress. Inside me was a limitless emptiness without a trace of hope.

One afternoon there was an air raid alert, which did not affect us a bit. The war was drawing to an end, but would we live to see it? Death would be a liberation from our suffering. Our watchmen suddenly disappeared. We were waiting for our salvation, but nothing happened. The day passed by the camp peacefully and with it returned our boundless hopelessness and the belief in the power of our invincible tormentors.

We were in Neustadt until January 1945. Our original group was now much smaller. The SS men began to watch us less, because they knew that there was no possibility for us to escape. We lived in little cabins, away from any other dwellings. These were actually round mud huts, windowless, with a diameter of about sixteen feet. We had to enter through a narrow door formed by several connected boards. There were fifty women in each of the little huts, which previously had been used as dog kennels. Through the middle of this little hut ran a potbelly stove, usually not functional. On the ground was straw which we brought from outside and that is how we existed. What misery! Already in September we suffered from frostbite and the winter was much worse. We were not dressed sufficiently and not fed well.

We marched to work each day and our job was building anti-aircraft bunkers. In many places we had to use heavy picks because the earth was frozen. The work routine and the daily kicks and beatings did not change. In the morning, following a coffee substitute and a slice of bread, they marched us to work. The rations were not sufficient to sustain the existence of working people. I was very undernourished and I grew weaker every day until I could barely pick up a spade. There was an SS man of Polish descent, who often was in charge of us. I once tried to talk to him. He did not like my friendliness. He did not like anybody in the camp, being a man without a soul, mean and vicious. He demonstrated these characteristics by starting to push me around and rough me up. Whenever he saw me resting, warming up, or moving to another place to work, he shoved me around with his rifle. I shook with fear whenever he approached me. Also, other SS men, with different ranks, some of them *obersturm-* or *untersturmführers*, used to come and give us orders. I could not understand their pathological hatred and their love of destroying the last strength of a person whom they knew they would finally slaughter.

The epidemic of typhoid fever broke out again. Some women looked like living skeletons, yet they forced themselves to keep up with the healthy ones. They did not want to be detected by the SS men who, as soon as they spotted a sick person, pulled him or her out of the room to be killed. The same work routine did not change: we went to work early in the morning and we came back in the evening. As we came home we got thin soup and a piece of bread. This was our dinner, which was supposed to give us enough energy for another day's work!

There was no place where we could wash. Early in the day we used to take some water and spill it on ourselves in the cold of the morning. We were always afraid that the SS men might see us and that they wouldn't like it, because this was not their order. They never told us that we should wash ourselves and we just had to follow orders. There was a very large latrine outside in the open, but it wasn't covered. It had open compartments for four people. It was very cold. At night, whoever had to go out, was scared to. For some time, we used to satisfy our needs in a pail in the little hut, which was not easy because we smelled the urine. Very often some women were so weak and unable to manage the situation that they used to relieve themselves in the straw, on which they slept. In the morning they removed the straw a little, and the straw got thinner and thinner every day. In the straw we also hid whatever little bread we could save from our meager breakfast. But under those circumstances one very often fell prey to some women who were stronger and managed to steal the hidden portion of bread. Each time there was some stealing of this kind, there were screams and cries, but it did not help. We tried to have a court inside the cabin but the stronger ones always prevailed and the rest of us had to accept their will.

Some girls developed quite a skill. When they were working, they somehow managed to dig up some carrots in the neighboring field, thus endangering their lives. Some girls managed to get potatoes. But the potatoes weren't cooked and those girls had to endure many great difficulties to get wood, make a fire, and then cook them. My friends were not in the same hut with me but they were very fortunate and they amassed quite a number of the raw vegetables. They dug a hole in the ground and they stored them there. When I asked them to share some with me, they refused. They told me to go and to try to find the vegetables myself. I was afraid that, should I be absent from work and go to the field, the Germans could catch me.

I did not feel like I could go on living any longer. The life was miserable and beyond human strength. A few times the SS men came and took some girls who then disappeared. We never heard of them again. One day the SS men came and told us that there was a big opportunity for whomever felt weak and would like to return to Stutthof. They asked if there were any volunteers. They looked us straight in the eyes. There were two older women in our cabin, who tried hard not to leave the hut, because of extreme fatigue. They pretended that they could go on fighting and starving in this camp. As they looked at everybody, I suddenly got a crazy idea. I felt that I could not take it any longer. I looked at the SS men and told them to take me, that I just couldn't work any more. What I meant to say was that I did not have clothes and shoes.

The others who were taken with me were stripped of their clothes. The Germans agreed. They took me from the room and brought me at night to a very large hut. There were fifty women, but there was still more space and empty bunk beds stuck in three rows one above the other. When I looked around, I was astonished to see that the place was lit by electric lights. I was very much impressed with the change of the environment in comparison with my old hut. Here there were many chronically ill girls—sick, swollen, and some just despondent, who felt that they couldn't fight any longer. They couldn't think rationally anymore, seeing death face to face. I was there for about two weeks. We did not get any clothes, but when a sick woman died, she was stripped of her clothes and shoes, and the girl next to her took proud possession of her belongings.

Then the SS men came in and said that they were going to examine us and decide what to do with us. Perhaps we could still work. They started to pound and ask who would like to leave that place. They looked at everybody. An SS man approached me and suddenly, it dawned on me that maybe this was our last hour and they were going to murder us. I looked at him bravely, straight into his eyes, and he said, "Oh, how did you get here? You can work; you are healthy and well. Get out of here." He took me away from the circle. There was another girl who decided to take my place and to stay behind; we traded places. They killed her later. Ever since I have had her on my conscience. If I hadn't left my place maybe she would still be alive and I would have died together with the others. Two days after we left Neustadt the SS men gathered all the girls in that group, told them to run, and shot them all, except for two.

CHAPTER EIGHTEEN

DEATH MARCH (OCTOBER, 1944)

In October 1944, our Death March began. We walked for miles every day. It was literally a real death march. My feet were sore from marching. For days we went without food. As I learned later the Germans were retreating and running away from the eastern front which was coming closer each day. When we came to a good road, like a main road, or to a crossing, we saw small groups of people, belonging to different nationalities, being transported. Sometimes the road became crowded with refugees and German soldiers. Nobody knew where they were going. Everybody was marching. Apparently they just did not use the trains any more. As we were marching, we were followed by two carriages with some clothes and provisions of the SS men. In the beginning the SS men permitted the weaker ones of our group who couldn't walk, to ride on the carriages, but soon decided not to show any favoritism and ordered the women to march, but the emaciated, weak victims couldn't march at this pace and they were executed.

The tempo of the march increased from hour to hour. On the road, while we were marching, we heard one or two shots, and a body fell. I remember there was a fourteen-year-old girl, tall and very good looking, with her mother. The people liked the daughter very much. The moment arrived when the mother couldn't walk. Disregarding her own weakness, the girl supported her, tried to make her keep up with us, but to no avail. A German finally came close to the mother, took his rifle and shot her in the temple. The daughter gazed into her mother's glassy eyes, trying to pick her up and to move her shoulders. Then she broke out in a cry, giving vent to her grief. At that moment, I felt as if I needed my mother's protection, but she was not there. I felt as if I knew what the daughter was going through. I had been constantly thinking of my mother and, through spiritual communication, praying for her help, hoping that she was still alive. I wanted to give the young girl my words of compassion and my arms in support, but I was too weak and too scared. I only swallowed my tears. I walked at some distance from her. Two days later we suddenly heard a shot. The SS men had killed the girl because she was so grief stricken that she couldn't walk any farther. I could never erase from my mind the picture of that young victim and of the creatures with human appearance, but worse than sharks, who were responsible for her death.

 I walked quite nicely, but the wind was howling and I was very cold. The cruel winter was upon us and the women were wasting away in hunger and frost. Listening to their weeping, one could have one's doubts about their survival and when their final hour would come. I just had some rags on my legs. I did not have shoes, and I hoped all the time that I would find some. We starved. The hunger, the thirst and the fatigue were indescribable. Some exhausted people without a ray of hope in their eyes, died or, not being able to keep up the pace with the rest, were kicked and killed by the SS men. We understood that we were all marked for death, but what was the reason to die through agonies of starvation and cruel beatings! There was only an occasional wail.

At night we usually slept in the fields and, when we were lucky, in a large barn, wherever we could find a place. The stronger girls found the better, more comfortable places. They used to kick me and hit me so that they would have more room and that they would be better located. But in general the common suffering drew us closer to each other. We were too weak to talk and there was usually only a silence of death.

I was successful in securing a pair of so-called *klumpen*, wooden shoes; they were quite small and they bruised my legs. When I walked, the icy snow came close to the surface of the shoes and stuck to the *klumpen* forming a wedge, so that it felt as if I were on a skate. Nobody paid any attention to the beautiful winter landscape. We were walking six or eight in a row and in the beginning the girls in my row supported me, because of my great tiredness. But everybody had to think of herself so that I had to stop every so often to cut off the ice. This was a very tragic race since nobody wanted to be at the end. As I stopped to take care of the shoes, the group would go farther on, and I was pretty close to the end of the column. This was the worst thing that could happen, because the girls left at the end would be considered weaklings, and they were constantly beaten and harassed by the soldiers and by the escort of German gendarmes. Often, if they only slacked a little and couldn't keep the pace, they were immediately shot. On several occasions I found myself at the end of the row frantically trying to manage to take care of my wooden shoes and rush to the front. I often lost my balance.

The death march, which stretched for very many miles, lasted a few weeks. We experienced human cruelty, sickness and hunger. Sometimes we raided a field of vegetables or sugar beets, which usually were fed to the cattle and had a very bitter taste, but we were happy that we had found something to eat. We learned to eat raw potatoes, which we diced into small pieces. We were very glad when we found them. On several occasions, unobserved, we raided a mound in the field, covering an excavation deep in the earth, like a little house, but we had to watch very carefully because the Germans would shoot whenever they saw us out of our row. Many perished at this time. We were not the only victims on that road. We heard from the people who were passing us, Frenchmen, Yugoslavians, Poles and Czechs, that nobody knew where they were taking us. Everybody was resigned. Even now, there was no letting down of German terror, based on utmost criminality and the trampling of human rights.

The men that we met on the road were even more emaciated than we were. They looked like skeletons. I remember we used to call them "mussulmen."

Finally, we came to a camp called Altamahost, in Pomerania. Here again, every morning, we were driven to work. In the beginning, the SS man in charge was fairly good, and he helped those of us who were sick with medications. He was a naturopath and knew medical therapy. His behavior proved that there were good-natured Germans, even among the SS men, but they were so rare that they stood out as the exception to the rule. In general, I saw hostility to the Jews more prevalent in the urban element and in the intelligentsia. But quite soon the situation changed and that man was replaced by other SS men who were very cruel and wild. They ordered us to get a complete haircut and we looked more like boys than like girls. We were unhappy. Many girls became sick with dysentery and typhus.

One day, I recall, I came from work and I was one of the last ones waiting for the soup. Not far from us lightning flashed and lit up the sky, and loud thunder crashed with a scary power. The first drops of an approaching storm started to pelt us and in a short time the rain came down hard. As I stood there an SS man came from behind and without any reason hit me with a hard object, perhaps a rifle. The world turned dark. The force of the blow threw me several yards. I fell to the ground and I fainted. The girls poured cold water on me, picked me up and brought me to my place. I developed a swelling and a small scar and I had terrible headaches for a while, but I had to go to work. On several other occasions the SS men mistreated us, pushed and knocked us down with their rifle butts.

There was a young SS man, perhaps only twenty-three or twenty-four years old, who once startled us by his sudden visit. He supposedly came to make an inspection. As we looked at him, standing at attention, he looked at faces of some girls and decided that they were not fit. They were too weak. I remember one girl, who was so weak that she was not able to move even faced with the danger of his inspection. He put her on the wheelbarrow and took four girls with him, two in front and two in the back, and he ordered them to push the wheelbarrow. I was one of the four. He brought us in the middle of the morning to a little wooded area covered with frozen water and mud. A shudder passed through my body when he ordered us, "Dig." We were to dig deep into the frozen ground to bury her, as he watched with suspicion. He yelled *los*—quicker. I recall how very miserable I felt. I used a pickax to break up the frozen ground. I couldn't believe that I had to participate in this, and I tried to get out of it. Even though I was very frightened of him, I told the young man that I didn't feel well. He squeezed my arm, almost raising me from the ground, and roared, staring at me, "Would you like to be buried with the girl?" I felt a chill and shook all over, understanding exactly what his intention was. I froze.

We heard only the sounds of the picks and our deep breathing before we made quite a deep hole in the ground. He pushed the girl, and as she stared at that incarnation of evil, she fell helplessly, without uttering even one word, into the hole. After he fired a single shot, he told us to cover her with earth. She was peacefully lying there, and from her mouth came the last gasps of life. I could not observe the last moments of her life and I was not too sure if she had expired before she was buried. I know that there were several other occasions that people were buried alive. When we finished, stricken with terror, none of us could look back toward the grave of the victim. The SS man stood over us motionless as if he was in communion with the devil. Finally, he ordered us to return down the dirty road to the camp. Even today, this incident shocks me anytime I recall it.

CHAPTER NINETEEN

LIBERATION

We were in this camp over two months. While there, we very often had the visits of the SS men from Stutthof, the mother organization. From there we were sent to Lauenburg in Pomerania. There was one camp for girls and two miles away there was a camp for men. I recall seeing very handsome SS men, who were in charge of the camp for men. They were occasionally assisted by attractive SS women, who used to come to our camp. They appeared to me like priests of a church of criminal bestiality. These women subjected us to treatment in a worse fashion than the men. They were very cruel and we could never understand how a woman could be put in charge of such barbarous work and how she could be so merciless.

More and more girls were dying of typhus and of starvation. Some were at the end of their endurance and had no hope to see the light of the dawn no matter when their turn to die would come. They badly wanted some food. No matter what happened and how the Germans performed on the front, here, with helpless, starved Jewish women, they were appearing as invincible devils. I was afraid that my end will also come soon.

As we worked outside we met some Germans who used to bring very thin sandwiches with them, maybe a fraction of an inch slice of bread, with butter and ham or salami. Rarely, they threw us such a sandwich, but we did not enjoy the trimmings; all we cared about was just the bread, and there was not enough of it. This was always our greatest dream. We promised ourselves that, if we ever survived the war, all we would ask was just to have enough bread. This would satisfy us because it would satisfy our hunger. We lost the entire desire for any fancy garnishing on the bread. For us the end of the war was still far away. We did not know what the next hour would bring.

I recall some Frenchmen working next to me. They told us that the front is nearing, that the Third Reich fights for its life and that we will soon be free. Their optimistic outlook was shaken when the SS men showed each day more cruelty. My head throbbed. I wanted to say something to them in French, but I had forgotten French entirely. It just left me blank and I was mad at myself remembering that once I had taught French. Typhoid fever and dysentery were decimating our small group. Every day one or two corpses were taken away and thrown on the pile of trash. Lord only knows what kept us going. We could hardly move. Often we prayed not to get up, just to die in our sleep and thus end our odyssey. The only thought that kept us going in those last days was the conviction that the violent Third Reich was near collapse. We didn't know any details about the English offensive, or where the Eastern front stood, but we felt that those were the last days of the totalitarian beast and we couldn't wait longer. But the question—who would live through this transition from slaughterhouse to liberation—was unanswered. Yet the voices became less subdued and there was more movement in our bunks

Finally, the day came when the German front collapsed. On a cold windy day in April, we were awakened, caught in a crossfire of shells and a barrage of machine guns. The distant bombing of the approaching Russian artillery woke us up from our desperate situation and rained fire upon the entire area. Explosions followed one another. A red glare covered the horizon. In the middle of the roar of the airplanes, closely exploding bombs shook the ground and our bunks. Some girls with a deadly look on their faces did not react to all this commotion because they were dying. Nobody could help them now. The others, no matter how weak they felt, jumped to their feet. There was a general excitation to the news of the approaching front. The danger of being caught in the front fire paled in comparison with the end of our hell. We did not share a word out loud, but our feeling was seen in the expression of our eyes. We were still afraid that, at the last moment, the scale of the battle might tip in the favor of the Germans and that the SS men might kill us all.

One of our buildings became engulfed in flames. The whistle of the shells flying over us was scary, but at the same time sounded like a beautiful symphony. The approach of the Russian artillery thunder grew distant once again and was replaced by the rattle of tanks and armored cars. Later clearly heard the clatter of the vehicles and then the hum of soldiers marching down the road. After a short battle between the Germans and the oncoming Russian troops, followed by a volley of rifle shots, the small gate of our camp fell and we left the compounds. Our watchmen disappeared. The Nazi shooting stopped.

When the volley of the intense gunfire stopped, we braved a glimpse through the door. The front passed the camp without causing any casualties. Seagulls and ravens began to fly overhead and they became closer to our hearts than those who belonged to our own species and called us sub-humans. Suddenly we were awakened from our long nightmare. We felt that the moment had come to sing and to shout and to celebrate our liberation, but we were too weak.

How did we receive our new freedom? We were in a daze. Barely moving, we offered support to the ones who were not able to take a step. We pushed those who were already written off into wheelbarrows, and then we went to face the new reality. Our minds were like a vacuum, our hearts empty of any desires. Yet we could not control our emotions. For the first time, since we had entered the ghetto and were tossed from one camp to another, we were free people who were not exposed to constant beatings, hunger and cold, without the barbed wire surrounding us. The armed SS men and their vicious dogs which jumped us were gone. They made a sudden cowardly escape. We realized that we were the lucky ones to greet the new world, that the majority was either killed by the Germans or succumbed to illness and hunger. We felt at that moment as if we were animals who had survived the evil human species. We remained taciturn, because there were no words capable to describe our emotions. Our story was expressed in a complete silence.

There was only one big piercing thought on our minds: to get some food, immediately and enough of it. On the streets, ecstatic Russian soldiers offered us sweets and cigarettes amid laughter and songs, but we were mute. The women were too weak to greet the jubilant Russians, who couldn't believe that we had experienced this misery. Since I knew some Russian, I was chosen to welcome our liberators. After I finished, an officer approached me and said in Russian: "Marusia, ty nasha," which means: "Marie you are one of ours," and he gave me a little fur coat.

Then I thought: Who are we? Where were we to go? Whom did we have to turn to? Our old world did not exist anymore. Empty feelings could not balance the physical, long awaited, dreamed of freedom. The inferno was over, the misery and terror came to an end; frightful days and sleepless nights filled with pain were no longer with us.

We were overcome with relief. It was almost too much to bear. I felt broken physically, but my quivering Jewish spirit of love and justice was not affected. My soul shook in a tremor that affected my highest values in relationship to men and to God, but it would never be conquered, never.

We went on an eating spree that lasted three days. With the German homes and especially, the basements, laden with enormous slabs of abandoned meat, our feast was a royal one. Many girls got sick and had to go to the hospital. Seven girls took up housekeeping in a four-room house. We burned our old striped clothes and put on brand-new outfits that we found in the streets and in the closets of the abandoned houses after taking a thorough bath.

Many new people arrived in town; they were also ex-inmates of the German concentration camps. We had a new wave of sickness. Shortly after I received the fur jacket from the Russian officer I started to feel sick. I suspected that a louse was hidden in that fur and had infected me. But there was a general epidemic of typhus, which took its toll. I was one of the first to fall victim to it. There is an entry on August 16, 1945, in the books of the local hospital that states that I died of typhus. I was amazed to learn this about five weeks later when, after a hard bout with death and full recovery, I took a job in the same hospital as a supervisor of the internal medicine ward.

Gradually, I gained peace of mind and most of all my health and my physical strength. Lauenburg changed its name to Lembork, as it was now occupied by the Poles. Now I could live in a nice, spacious, small-town Gothic home, having a job in the hospital, and I advanced in my job. But I was restless. I soon met a girl from the same town where my sister and her husband lived, and she told me all about their tragic last moments. I decided to go back to Warsaw and try to find the last living remnants of the once great Polish Jewry.

My visit to Warsaw was short. I was heartbroken. I walked the streets of Warsaw, the streets of my school days, childhood, and dreams, where I knew every little stone, and I cried like a baby. All that was left were ruins, piles of dirt, or rocks. All the past—family, relatives and friends—was in ruins also. Should I put a curtain on the past, erase it and forget? I was offered a good lucrative job in Warsaw. They badly needed well-educated people to replenish the losses caused by the cruel war. After careful consideration, I said "no" and left for Lodz. I could not bear to live and work in Warsaw on the ruins of the past. In Lodz I met one of my previous friends, an inmate of the camp, and went to live with her. We were six girls living together in a small apartment. We slept on the floor and the girl's father, a shoemaker, who had also come back from a concentration camp, was our provider.

My prayers and cherished hope, that somebody from my family would have survived, and the search for relatives and friends, brought sad results. My parents had perished on Mila 18, in the heroic fight of the Warsaw ghetto; each of my brothers and sisters found death under different circumstances. Only the two first cousins, who had left Warsaw with us, miraculously avoided the Nazi ax and survived the war. They were carted out by the Russians in March 1940, and transported to the forests of Wologda. They suffered hunger and extreme cold, but they survived the war.

I could not live in the land that had swallowed all my loved ones. My old world did not exist anymore.

I was choking in the new Poland. I needed fresh air to breathe. There was no purpose for me there. In search of a new life, I left Poland with tears and vague hopes. What would the future bring? I went into a great unknown, but I knew there would be no persecution and terror. An old friend broke down in tears when I told him how I had survived the Vilno ghetto and twelve camps: Vievis, Milejgany, Zezmarai, Kaiserwald, Panevezys Flugplatz, Siaulai, Gefangerlager Kaunas, Stutthof, Steinort, Neustadt, Altamahost, and Lauenburg. It was six years since the war had swept me away from a normal family life in Warsaw, which now became but a dream. I lost all that I loved in the indescribable misfortune of the war.

Looking back at my own and at the recorded human history of six millennia, we ask, where was morality with man constantly killing man? True, there was Mount Sinai and the Ten Commandments, but it was a reaction to the pre-existing and to the following immorality.

CHAPTER TWENTY

A New Beginning

The train spilled hundreds of people, alone and with the tragic past behind them, on the Austrian soil. A young man came closer to me and in flawless Polish asked: "May I help you carry your bundles?" I answered, "Yes," and he is still helping me carry the burden of life: he is my dear husband. We lived together in Austria in DP (Displaced Persons) camps in different locations for five years. We were terribly poor, had not much to wear, and the food was rationed—small packages from the Joint Distribution Committee—we lived in a room eight by ten feet, first with one, later with two babies, but happy. We learned to appreciate each other and most of all to enjoy the magic world of freedom.

In 1950, we came to the United States after a small door in the immigration policy of the United States was opened for us. We came to the States penniless, but our struggle for survival was over. We found a home, job, opportunities, and joy in the New World. Eventually, we put down roots in Claremont. I never really regained my previous health completely. The war experience left me with a heart neurosis, frequent headaches, and arthritis, but I am thankful to God for preserving me and permitting me to be alive. We started to explore the world with joy, like travelers from another planet, and constantly wondered how we had both been able to survive the ghetto and what followed. I was a veteran of twelve camps and of the death march, and Joe escaped death on so many occasions. It was as if we were reading somebody else's story. We started to learn to live like other people around us and to give praise for the greatest gift, life.

Looking at the mountains and the blue sky, I expressed my happiness with the peace and the unexpected miracle that we had found here. I felt like a flower. The children would remember for the rest of their lives the gentle peace that we found here. The rented house did not have any air conditioning, and the summer heat, which extended into the autumn, was suffocating. At that time I still had tremendous energy. I would bring the children to and from school, and then go shopping. I would cook, wash, and bring the children to scouting. And then I still could find time to read them books and tell stories, which would penetrate the delicate reaches of their imagination.

Our children were growing up in fabulous surroundings. I spent a lot of effort in their proper upbringing. Joe helped me enormously, even though as I see it from the perspective of time, he was too obsessed with the Holocaust, to which he devoted too much time. He probably neglected the present world for the one that we had lost. I was a bond and the glue connecting the two worlds in which he existed, and served as an inspiration to live in reality. He said that he needed my serene companionship and enthusiasm for children and for the exultation for life.

In the meantime, Joe was successful in his practice of allergy, and quite a number of local physicians were his patients or sent their families to him for medical care. He became a member of the faculty at Loma Linda University Medical School. There he once met Rabbi Heschel, who had been invited as a guest speaker. He continued some clinical and laboratory research, the result of which was published in medical journals. I accompanied him a number of times to social affairs of the medical staff at Loma Linda. He was happy to introduce me to some of his acquaintances. Otherwise, except for one or two times, I accompanied him to medical conventions, whenever he went.

We enjoyed the friendship of a number of local people. Richard grew up very fast and was taller than his parents and went through his Bar Mitzva and graduating class. We were visited by Stas, his wife Beatrice and by a number of friends from out of town and a by few local friends.

In the beginning I kept Joe's records and wrote his correspondence, but finally I could stay home and he got a secretary.

I remember vividly those times. In spite of his hard life, Joe has a sweet, funny disposition. He likes a good laugh and makes jokes. A typical day in Joe's practice was associated with a lot of fun. After kissing me goodbye, he entered his car and moved his briefcase with papers and towels to the side. He had been taking them from home for his noon exercises at the spa. He would correct his tie, his hair, he would whistle some melody and he would speed up to the office. Sometimes colleagues and friends would pass him in the car and wave to him and he waved back a number of times. When he entered the office, there was already a group of children wit waiting with their mothers. Usually Mondays were hectic. In addition to his usual day schedule, there was a spill over of illnesses that had been contracted during the two days of the weekend. "Good morning, good morning," he greeted everyone, nodding his head, waving hands, and smiling. A few children answered with a funny expression that he used with them. "What's new in Kalamazoo? Hi Mickey Mouse. How are you sonny boy? Stop your monkey business!" Years later a young man would come from the back and touch his shoulder; he would have troubles recognizing the moustache of the young man who would say, "What's new in Kalamazoo, sonny boy?" This put him in a real good mood, but to top it all, the first patient whom he had just examined, a five-year-old boy, was so happy that Joe had talked his mother out of giving him an injection that he spontaneously blubbered. "Doc, you are such a fine man, I love you so much, but you are going bananas." This made his day.

After we got a secretary, he usually called me from the office at least once or twice during the day to find out how I was doing and how the children were.

Joe did not like any surgery unless it was unavoidable, and therefore he opposed my decision to strip my veins, which really did not bother me and created only a cosmetic problem. I was in good health. One time, I was even able to climb to the top of Mount Baldy with him. I did not like my varicose veins acquired during the pregnancy. I had continually nagged him about having surgery for my varicose veins. He finally agreed to my going ahead with the surgery, and that nearly became a fatal decision. Immediately afterwards, I developed a massive pulmonary embolism which almost killed me. My surgery was, incidentally, performed by a friend who was also a patient of his. He asked Joe to assist him during the surgery. The treatment of heparin injections for almost a year was followed by oral anticoagulants tablets. I almost died and since then I developed changes in my lungs, which contributed to my illness for a period of years. At that time, we realized our vulnerability and we tried to vocalize the feelings which we had before. I made notes.

A number of years later, a nearly fatal series of car accidents caused by other drivers took place. One of those accidents left me with rib fractures and internal injuries. Since that time, I started having serious heart disease, with a coronary artery occlusion in 1994.

What I am going to write here has nothing to do with my husband or our relationship. In all frankness, I succumb to pressures that are all around me and within me. The ones around me painted a beautiful aura of stimulation, satisfaction, and sharing like experiences. The real trials and tribulations of the family of man would, I knew, usher us through this together. People from all walks of life and of different moods and attitudes caused us to become acutely aware of the magnitude of what had happened. The pressures within me are because I'm an incurable dreamer. I'm also an optimist against all odds. To hope is to dream in spite of the evils of the twentieth century, of my dark past experience and of the wreckage of my illusions, I believe in the ongoing process of morality, which I am trying to discover in others.

After surviving the war's atrocities, I try to make sense of my emotions and of the psychological jungle I have entered. There is no doubt that the years of the Holocaust molded our views of the world, of God, and of sin. If there is any sin, it is the refusal to live up to one's moral potential. Judaism must come from the roots of our souls, from what we feel and how we act. In this respect I think in a similar way as my husband does. From him I learned to change my attitude to God. It is refreshingly new and it seems to me to be intellectually stimulating. Our disappointment in history should be directed not to God, but to people, he says. The question is not where was God during our Golgotha, but where was man. No structured religion means much without a moral behavior and our ultimate challenge as a religious people is to resurrect this transcendent idea. So what is the definition of God, if he is not our protector? Joe says that He is the Creator. Why then should we love Him, if He does not love us, if He did not play a role in the history of the Holocaust? Do not expect anything from God; in particular, don't believe that a prayer to Him will give you what you desire, says Joe.

Prayer as an expression of love forms one and makes one feel better. The feeling of unlimited love for somebody is something that cannot be described by any adjectives. It leaves you with a sensation of satisfaction and perhaps of happiness greater than the love for those that you could describe, like your parents, spouse or children, according to Joe. He also says that a prayer brings one into unity with the unknown God and brings strength, even as it seems to be talking to oneself.

For me, as for most people, this might be hard to understand, but my husband insists that a prayer expressing love affects the praying person in the right way and that it changes him without the need to reach God, who is acting in history. He believes that without praying to God, he would not have been able to survive the war. He is still praying daily. Morality, he says, must rule interhuman relations and be based on love and justice. I am bringing this up to point to the fact that the most devastating experience and the greatest suffering will not necessarily break a strong spirit.

Scientists try to unravel the secrets of the world and I ask myself what we might hope to gain without the moral application of their achievements. Again, I see, like my husband does, a crisis of morality, which calls for emergency help in changing of attitudes. That help must be used as an aid in the disappearance of the paranoia in inter-human relations, to foment love and to be conscious of the fact that we are all brothers, rather than in the further explosion of technology and in the constant improvement of destructive push-button weapons.

I want to come close to people to see how they live and experience their tribulations, even though there are not many who are interested in the Holocaust. Those that are, are trying to understand how I survived and are more interested with my person, rather than with the mechanics of the unprecedented historical events in my life. They still cannot face the human capacity to do evil.

With regard to my husband, I want to be open and to find the key to his sometime selectiveness. I believe that this outreach to individual people is not important to him as his entire mind is directed towards bigger things. I tried to learn to communicate, to enhance and to enrich our marriage. We should not only experience our feelings, but we should mentally register them and share with others. A physical and spiritual relationship is one thing and a good clear analysis is another.

My feelings of happiness are different from Joe's. He should try to experience my feelings with all my senses and to grow closer to me. Being lonely, like being lost in the forest, I sometimes feel isolated. I'm concerned when Joe is not well. We did not yet reach the end of the tunnel and it is virtually scary. We accept each other in order to make our marriage better.

Joe, you are somebody that I can depend on, you are reliable and it gives me a sense of security to be around you. I can lean on you and I draw my strength from you. I think that I am fairly open, loyal, and honest. I don't go for the small talk or attempt to be all lovey-dovey. That's too often seen in other marriages and is part and parcel of some marital relationships I am very thankful that we both share similar concerns. As Jews we are proud of who we are; we have strong feelings and share a dedication to just causes and love and care for our children. True, we would like them to be a symbol of perfection, but after all, we walk on the ground and see that they have made some giant steps to get an education to come to the place where they are right now.

There is no doubt that I am a complex person. I never envy others and I never wanted to be like the rich or physically beautiful. I had my own standards. I was always searching, driving hard to get to know more. I care about others; moreover, I am a compassionate person and I try to help. And I'm open to changes any time I see the reason. I have my weak points, I am somewhat disorganized, I am somewhat forgetful, I am very fragile, and I don't forget enough adversities. But on the other hand, I suffered so much that one cannot forget. I'm sometimes shy, perhaps more than I should be, but I try to stay on as straight a road as I can. However, Joe feels that, if he takes a stand after long consideration, he always has to be right. My insecurities very often prevent me from defending my stand. I try to be an open, honest mother and wife. Though I consider that I am giving of myself and considerate, I would like to help others more and share with others whatever my abilities permit.

I should not so easily unburden myself to Joe. I have to realize that he is under tremendous pressure. I want to help him, to ease and to comfort him in his spiritual pain. He likes to share that pain with me. I wish to have a real talent and to be more creative than I am to help him more. The Holocaust killed something in me forever. I had to rebuild my shattered life, physically and spiritually. I did not buckle under and I felt as though I was not defeated, which I believe is good. And I wonder how, after so many camps, I got the fortitude to do so.

Joe is my escape, my fountain of strength. I love him so dearly and often I don't understand him. He lives somewhere else, perhaps too much absorbed with his job and his responsibilities to his inner calling and his pursuit to be perfect. He has so many talents and abilities, that it makes you mad sometimes that God did not spread it among many people.

I am so imperfect, fragile, frightened, and often insecure. I don't know how to change. I know that I have to be supportive as a wife and I try to do my best. Our marital love is a true joy, even though not always expressed verbally. Your job, Joe, your involvement in constant study, research, and reflections are not helpful in our marriage, but ours is a unique marriage. Physical death will not be frightening to me, except that it's going to deprive me of you. Now, the pursuit of good health should be revered and respected, and we both practice it. When I'm not well, one good word from you helps me move mountains.

Work is very important to you and you do a great job, but you must not pay too big a price. You must attempt to cut some corners and try to get away from it all from time to time. Try to enjoy life more and escape the pressures of everyday life. You gave the children everything you possess and that is your best quality. Let us hope that they will not only appreciate all the input and live a good, honest life and go down the road of righteousness, but that they will develop your values even farther.

Even though our marriage is very good and we are so close to each other, I wish that we could gain an even greater understanding for each other. Sometimes, I feel like closing the door to myself and staying only with myself. I feel that I am alone, helpless to change, because of the overwhelming pressures of the world. I sometimes get steamed up and I know I can hurt you or inadvertently stop your work. You are showing me more interest and understanding than I expected. I know that you have no time for trivia, so I brood alone until I can overcome the crisis. Before, I used to have a good cry and this gave me relief. But now my eyes are dry and I try to overcome the frustration that I feel. I think I have changed somehow, maturing and now being able to understand things that were beyond my reach before. I never feel defeated because I can always spring back. It is a different story when one hurts me, but even then, the pain does not remain with me for too long.

Like you, Joe, I have a deep feeling for justice. And when we came to the Promised Land for the first time, I felt joy, pride, serenity, and an overwhelming satisfaction that Jews had finally become builders of their own destiny. When the children left home and I was alone and decided to go to Chaffey College, I felt understood and appreciated and gratified when I brought home the report card of being on the Dean's List. And I know that you shared in my happiness and you were proud of my achievements. There are times that I want to tell you so much how I feel. I am filled up with a sense of knowing and simultaneous feelings of inadequacy, fright, and insecurity. I feel this particularly when you are called at night or leave for a meeting and come back very late. I am there at the window, crying my heart out, full of doubts, full of disquieting thoughts of what could happen. In order to understand me one has to be in my head. There is no life without you and everything falls apart when I don't feel your strong arms close to me and I am left alone to brood

I am writing these words with a renewed feeling of stronger love for you, my husband. I don't have the talents and abilities of the great women of letters and poetry. And most of all, as people often do, I have difficultly putting my words into feelings. On the other hand, I feel that I have the same capacity for love and a greater reservoir for tender, warm emotions than others.

We met under very unusual circumstances, when our entire existence after the catastrophe of the Holocaust was one big question mark. Two people, solitary souls alone in the world and abandoned by all the western and not so western societies, met by sheer accident. Call it a spark of fate. At that time, I knew little about where I was going and what would be the course of my future. I was confused, alone with myself, but anxious to forge ahead and find the impossible dream, a new life in the world. I really did not know what my future was going to be like; all I knew was that I must make a fresh start. If I had to find a place for myself in the great vast desert of post-war life, I had to continue my existence as a Jewish woman and build a new world on the ashes of the old rotten existence of deprivations, suffering, killing and constant agonizing from the brutalities of the Nazi era. There was not yet much thought about marriage, a man in my life and sharing life together. This came suddenly. I awakened from the bad dream of the previous six years and suddenly I had a feeling that all my body was stirred up, saying: you can't go on living alone, you have a lot to give of yourself, and in return you will receive the most beautiful gift, man's love. You will blossom, you will feel your blood tingle, your head will begin to spin. The whole world will be full of happiness and joy. You would start drinking from the well of life, the intoxicating elixir, you would be drunk with new strength. Your limbs, your head, your body were full of him and before long I had realized that it was love. What a good, precious feeling I wanted to share, to have you close to me, to hear both our hearts beating in unison and most of all learning about all the mysteries of your world. I was wanted, needed, and loved. Many years passed and you were my husband, the father of our children, my lover and supporter, my rock and my defender.

You were the father that I never felt I had. Oh, how I missed having a father close to me as a child, caressing me and even spoiling me with his tenderness. You succeeded to sooth my pain when you were near. Although this is not an accusation because you gave me much more than I gave you in return, being burned up by the fire within you to succeed, to be a provider and to do well in your profession to the best of your ability, you were unfortunately away from us a great deal.

Your job as a physician absolved you completely and our marriage succeeded. Now one thought invades my mind and begs to be brought to the fore. How little we appreciate each other in life. We put burdens under our feet and make life difficult for both of us. How true it is that couples fight sometimes and bicker, but when we are no longer around, we realize how unjust we were. We forget to tell our spouse how much that person meant to us. Let us open our minds more and realize that there is a lot of goodness in each other, so we can enjoy our life more while we are on this side of heaven. I want to go on living, of course. There is so much beauty in life and I love the unknown. There is no end to our experimentation, to the great discoveries I find in you and in the ever-changing world.

As far as our relationship, I want to rediscover in you many things that I missed. I want to appreciate you more, not to take you for granted, to protect you with all my heart and my mind, if you would only let me. I want you to keep away all thoughts of guilt you might have so that I might keep you happy, relaxed, and satisfied, most of all physically and spiritually well.

I want to redefine many things within myself and to be reborn. I want to start to work on a new me. Is there any question as to why we must go on living? We are not tired of living, for if I were, I would not plan to finish my life. God gave us life and I will stay here on earth as long as he wants me to stay. There is so much unfinished business that we both have. I love you, I love you, I love you, and there is no one but you. Whom do I turn to when you are not around? There is no surrogate or replacement for you. You are the constantly changing world, churning and stirring and enriching yourself and all those around you. You are very tender and good to me. You are very generous, sometimes you are shy and sparse with showing your love, but I understand that this is your upbringing. But you are the greatest, you are irreplaceable and nobody is like you.

In the beginning of our relationship you needed me very much. You were all alone like I and you and I had the same dreams. You helped me to continue living and being what I am today and what I dreamed to be tomorrow. It matters not that you are rough and uncut in some places, because you are beautiful, warm, loving and mine. I would not change you for all the riches in the world. I hope that I satisfy your needs and I am a star in your eyes and you derive joy and pleasure from our relationship. You are tender and sweet. If sometimes I do not live up to your expectations, it is because I inhabit a different planet, I am deadly tired and sick. You are beautiful, sensitive like the fragile flowers in the field of spring. I wish only to hear from you if and how much our commitment to each other needs strengthening. Perhaps all will come our way. I probably demand too much from you and from life. Take what life offers you and build a magnificent garden of flowers with different shapes and colors. Sip the fragrance of the garden slowly so that you will know you stand strong on both of your feet. No, there must not be an impossible dream. Maybe then we will discover God in ourselves. We have to be aware of how important it is to give and to receive. Fill up my senses, come and be always with me, let me always love you. We had an awareness that we are a team. For each of us there is a special dose of love. We have to try to rekindle our love for each other every day, every moment We have to see the experience of growth in each other and rediscover each other constantly and the beauty which surrounds us; I will always find you among the flowers. In my apprehension, getting back to the real world after a period of long suffering, I was tuned in to Joe and I wanted this to last forever. We went on trips together, he took me on his walks and I became a part of him. I am trying to be good to you, Joe, and I want our marriage to last, as it is, forever; I would like to be less apprehensive and to trust you even more than I do. Take me on walks and on trips with you and let us be closer. Let us create a oneness of feelings. I will give you as much love as I can, and you will teach me how to give more. I sometimes want to be caressed, hugged, lost in your embrace. I want to hear your voice, your whisperings, softly saying, "I love you." I want to see in your eyes the fire of desire. I want to get to taste your kisses and to smell your body, your lips, and your tender hands. I feel rejuvenated around you. Perhaps, what we need badly before we fall into oblivion, is to come closer to each other, to support each other morally even more than we do now and to give strength and help to each other.

When I want to do something good, I don't think twice. Something takes over my head, my heart, my whole being. I know I must do it because the person is in need or because there is no one else to fill the gap.

It started in New York with Molly, who was wonderful, self-effacing, giving and generous. I felt that I should give her a slice of me, so that she knows that somebody cares, somebody thinks about her and about her needs. You saw right away inherent dangers in my behavior and you said that nothing good would become of it. "You will only get hurt because this woman is paranoid," you said. Perhaps, because of that, she knew so little love. I felt that I should do something for her.

When our children were growing up, I often wanted to do something good for others, but you saw me always getting into trouble or getting hurt. First and foremost, you wanted to protect me, so I did not really do as much as I wanted. It gave me great pleasure to help the mother with six children, two of which were considered mentally retarded. I went there regularly, twice a week, until they moved away. I knew that I was wanted and I was needed. I also went to visit the other mother with seven children. What an experience! Then there was the place where we went together, to Chino Men's Prison, where I was so anxious to see you with me. Remember how we felt when you went with me, how proud of you I was. You did a beautiful job and we got some insight into the psyche of fellows who came in conflict with the law. I always tried to invite single, solitary people who had no family to our seders, as well as some Christian friends, who desired to get an understanding and feeling of Passover. Weren't you happy having them with us during the Passover so that they could share and celebrate with us the memory of the great events of our history?

I hope that someday, you will find more joy in your own life and you will be able to work less, have less tension, and be more willing to get interested in the life of others. So many people are waiting for your help. Are we failing and are we following the ethical principles that we preach? I would not speak about this and direct it to you, but I see it for myself. I need it as long as we communicate with the world around us. We have to make a balance sheet, and the balance sheet should not be done once in a lifetime. It has to be done on a daily basis. I feel a little restless; I feel somewhat as if I did not live up to the great expectations of a person who has had my past experiences.

I told you, Joe, that I felt somehow inadequate. I wanted to understand more and better about our obligations as survivors to other human beings. You had an easy answer: "Everything is fine as long as our marriage is in good shape; we cannot resolve all the problems of the world." You did not like the constant kissing and looking into each other's eyes, especially if done publicly. You said, "I can kiss you whenever I like and whenever I feel like it, but I won't do it for export. I don't like exhibitionism in any form."

We dispensed with this problem and decided that our great promise was to build a healthy community by using our marriage as an example. Joe is much better than I. He is the brain trust in our family. We are searching deeper for a new world of ideas to spring from. Only through inner growth and spiritual ability can we improve, and our hunger for want can be satisfied. I am searching for the tune, for the music to my ears that will permit me to better understand the sensitivities of life of the contemporary scene. Our marriage cannot be improved, but it can be made more pleasant. We are still in our first love, which cannot be duplicated. This love never stopped. I am happy with the present state of affairs and I don't need an avalanche of new ideas. I want and ask only for very small changes.

Our life is beautiful, inspiring, and I cannot imagine a better one. When I ask Joe if he would like some great changes, he said that our lives taught him humility and appreciation of his partner. He wants to stop briefly to see how life can be changed and how we might develop a common appreciation of each other. These ideas were deeply rooted in him, he says. I have only to reaffirm their existence. He said that our marriage is based on complete trust and strong bonds, which do not need strengthening. There must only be a mild polishing of a certain roughness. Like old people around me, I want to achieve inner peace and tranquility. I want to see things realized in tender love, not only between us, but in the community. The mystical power of love binds us together and what we need is only some polish. While the chemicals of our bodies change, we realize that the lasting effect of our emotions lasts longer than our biological existence.

Our friends frequently ask me how we met and how we generated such endless love for each other. We met as refugees on Austrian soil. It was as natural as when the waves infuse each other in oneness. It was neither a blissful nor a beautiful seduction. It felt as if somebody had predestined this moment as our reunion rather than our first meeting. It was as if we had known each other before and were happy to meet again. There was no long courting; it was instantaneous. There was more than the devotion to each other. It was complementation of each other. It felt as if we were separated and now were getting back together, and nature glued us back in one block. I was not a partner. This came later with the children. I was a part of him. I needed protection, and he needed somebody to protect. I was terrified by my losses, and anxious. He was still fighting to stay alive. I was on the defensive, he on the offensive. I was running from the past. He was chasing it.

In my need of support and protection, I sometimes called him 'Daddy,' or, in Polish, 'Tatka.' He called me 'Baby,' or 'Mama,' during moments of closeness and confidentiality. Otherwise, we called each other by our names, Joe and Marie. He told me that he always saw in me a spiritual innocence and trust in him, an outreach of my nature, which he needed like daily bread.

Later, when I kept our newborn baby in her white outfit with the background of the dark slopes of the Alps, Joe described our silhouettes as appearing angelic to him. I love children so very much. I also like plants and flowers. When I was very sick, I asked Joe to cut them and bring them to me.

I feel a part of God's creation and a part of you, dear Joe, and in my prayers I long to unite with the Almighty.

CHAPTER TWENTY-ONE

FROM THE ABYSS TO THE SUMMIT

This is the story of how we met. I will not go into all the details, but this is how our lives unfolded at that time. It was a late afternoon when cars spilled us, Jewish refuges from Poland, out on to the railroad station at Linz, in Austria, in 1945. We came in separate transports, smuggled out by the organization known as Bricha. His group arrived earlier and was waiting for additional people before being directed to our new displaced persons camp, Bindermichel. Since he had practically nothing to carry, he offered me his help. I had nine packages, which I had brought from Warsaw.

It was love at first sight, which grew over many years and cemented our relationship into a symbiosis. He told me that my warm blue eyes and blond hair charmed him-. When he asked me why I had cut my hair so short, I explained that they were cut in the concentration camp and they were just now growing back.

Our quarters were next to each other, and later on, we worked as volunteers in the camp, and this strengthened our romance. With the approval of a female Irish officer, we organized a school for the children. During the war, this group of children had lived with their parents in Soviet Russia. Joe became the school principal and I became one of the teachers. People who arrived in our camp later brought news about further persecutions and killings of Jews who miraculously had returned from concentration camps to Poland. Joe started to collect the materials of those eyewitnesses, running away from our homeland, Poland, and after he confirmed them by other sources, he used them as the basis of his first book, *SOS—The Cry of the Democracy for Help*.

In the evening, we walked to the theater in Steyr, and we were drunk with freedom and the beautiful Austrian nature. The people were very polite, cultural, and full of life. I wondered how the same people produced the members of the Gestapo and of the highest echelon of the Nazi Party, including Hitler. Since Joe's home town, Przemysl, was in Galicia, a part of Austria-Hungary before World War I, and because his father had lost his eyesight during that war, while serving in the Austrian Army, he felt some loose connections with this country. Austria had been divided into four zones of occupation after the war, and we lived in the English one.

One afternoon, our supervising Irish officer invited Joe for a walk. She asked him about the food and living conditions in camp, and then suddenly she asked him about his relationship to me: was he seriously involved with me, and did he intend to marry me? When he told her that he indeed had this plan in the nearest future, she cut short their walk.

Soon thereafter, an opportunity opened to move to another DP camp in Bad Gastein. We grabbed this chance, not knowing what to expect. When we arrived there, we thought that somebody had prepared a paradise for us. Here, our courtship got stronger, and we married on August 10th, 1945. Since there was no rabbi available, we undertook to get married in a civil ceremony. We needed witnesses whom we found outside the court: a Jew and an Austrian. This was the entire audience for our vows.

We left the court as happy as could be, and we mingled with the Austrian public, which was behaving as if the Second World War were never known to them. The town was not touched by the war, nor were the villages surrounding it, while our world had disappeared, destroyed by the same people who now laughed and had a good time with their children. I thought and compared our existence with theirs, even while I was supposed to rejoice, pick up the pieces, and start a new life.

We lived in one of the hotels. Since it was considered to be a Displaced Persons' camp, we had our camp police, which checked that only members enter. I remember how, because of my appearance, with blond hair and blue eyes, I was stopped on one occasion by a policeman and Joe had to vouch for the fact that I was Jewish and a member of the camp.

As husband and wife, we dreamed about a steady place and a family. In the new camp, we made friends and started to work. Joe was writing for the camp bulletin, and I, with my law degree, became a member of the camp court. He spent a part of his time on writing his first booklet, *SOS*, which he was in a hurry to finish. He had his past experience with writing. In the ghetto, he had lost his memoirs at the time before the Nazis transported them to Auschwitz. We found enough time to walk a lot and to climb the Alps. On those walks, Joe befriended Sonia, a nurse who told him how she had survived in the Russian Partisan group of Medvedevcy. He made notes of her reports and used them in his book, published in 1993, *The Embers of Michael*.

SOS had originally been written by Joe in Polish, but a man by the name of Zurach, a partisan from Lithuania, helped him with translating the book into Yiddish. He was hurrying because an English-American commission, which was to study the question of Jews, particularly Jews in the displaced persons camps, was about to arrive. He wanted to be able to offer the members of the commission his book in order to point out how important it is to find a permanent homeland for the survivors, in view of the persecutions and killing of Jews in Poland. He worked on it day and night and finished it in time. Somehow, he got the needed money and went to a printer in Salzburg. Since there were no available Hebrew letters, the book was translated into Yiddish written in the Latin alphabet. He sold ten thousand copies in several camps. In Linz, Simon Wiesenthal, the famous Nazi hunter, helped him to sell a number of copies and brought a copy of the book to the Polish attaché, Jerzy Lec, in Vienna.

Now, since he had this project behind him, he wanted to make up for the lost time during the war and to finish his medical studies. He tried to get information about different universities.

Joe left for Innsbruck. Here, he was admitted by the polite, distinguished chairman of the admissions committee, Professor Lang, who, as Joe found out later, had been a former SS general. I wondered whether the man would be as polite to him as he was, if there was an independent Austria. This country was now occupied by the United States, United Kingdom, Soviet Union, and France. Innsbruck was in the French zone.

Joe was working very hard, communicating with me through the office of the local Joint Distribution Committee, an American organization, which supported us with some food rations. Since he came from another camp, he did not receive the rations. Therefore, he frequently worked hungry. I sent him bread once or twice, which became moldy. But even so, it served him well.

Incidentally, the chief officer of the Local Joint Distribution Committee was a German by the name of Schmeisner who, as we found out later, was a member of the Nazi Party, but at that moment pretended to be Jewish. One day, Schmeisner informed Joe that I had delivered a baby girl.

Joe figured that the news would complicate his decision to continue his medical studies. But the idea of extending our lives when our old world had died in the smoke of the crematoria was more important. As I told him later, I complained of an upset stomach to neighbors for a few days. It did not respond to home remedies, and when it got worse, they brought me to the hospital in Bad Hofgastein. Joe couldn't wait for the train to pull into the station at Bad Gastein, and he immediately took off by foot to Bad Hofgastein.

I was very happy to see him even though he was not with me during the delivery. He couldn't wait until the nurse brought in the baby with cheeks as beautiful as two peaches, with lively eyes, and clinging to him right away. This was Lillian.

We were elated to see in Lillian, in addition to the extension of our own life, a compensation for the lives lost during the war. Joe's love for me deepened and extended beyond my physical attraction right from the beginning. True, he told me that I was charming, intelligent, and stimulating, but for a man who had lost his world, I represented that world and was a bond with the past. I survived as he had, but by different means, hard to conceive by people who had not had our experience. Shortly thereafter, he told me, I had become a symbol of the Holocaust for him and a representative of the idea of the preservation of life and of its creative forces.

We both represented the enormous suffering inflicted on us by the Nazis. We both had survived incredible experiences against all odds. But there was a difference: Joe had showed some initiative in defending himself, while I, being totally passive, was tossed from one camp to another. I ended the war as a veteran of twelve camps, the last of which was the annihilation camp in Stutthof. Finally, I took part in the Death March. He had never been in a concentration camp, but he escaped death numerous times. And to answer the question of how each of us survived became, in the future, a philosophical challenge, which he had not been able to solve until much later, in spite of discussing the subject with clergymen and philosophers and consulting the literature. Was this a chance or a miracle? Or is a chance a miracle seen through the eyes of a believer?

We both felt contempt for the killers, but Joe additionally saw in it a universal conflict between good and evil and his active role on the side of good. He also felt that even if this part of his efforts gave insignificant results, he must warn the world about the dangers of human evil.

Later, the symbol of the Holocaust grew in his conception to incorporate a love of creation and of the Creator and thus, it unified the objects of his love: the past, the present and existence in general. When he kissed my neck and smelled my skin, he consciously embraced existence and the idea of the Creator. To protect that symbol became his deepest desire and holy duty. When we were hiking in the Alps or resting on the slopes of mountainous meadows, he said that I became confluent with nature, a part of it. He believed that God created beauty in a symbolic compensation for all our losses: those of our parents, family, friends, and of our People. He had a deep need to protect me, the object of his love, and I needed to be protected. In my openness and trust, I expressed this desire and strengthened his feelings. Our love for each other was based on friendship and that trust, which will last until the very end of our relationship. I attributed our strong marital bonds to this mutual need after our old world had been destroyed, and we had only ourselves. We had to pick up the pieces and start to carry on. Our mission was to create a new life and here was proof of our success: Lillian.

Joe told me that it was a constant wonder for him how my gentle disposition was not scarred by twelve camps and that my past experience had not affected my character whatsoever. But my body eventually felt it.

In the meantime, he studied hard to make up the time lost during the war. He frequently walked miles to the medical school, not having bus fare. There were many foreign students from the Soviet Bloc countries. He had no time for socializing with them, but he wondered frequently whether some of them had served the Nazis. He soon found out that the Nazis hadn't suddenly evaporated with the defeat of Germany, and that the Nuremberg Trial of a small number of individuals was only a symbol of punishment. He had some hints that he was not surrounded by angels. He soon found out that in addition to his distinguished pathology professor, there were others on the faculty who also had a less than pristine past. His professor of surgery, a jolly old fellow, always smiling and joking, was an SS major. Later, this Professor Breitner became the head of the Neo-Nazi Party in Austria. There was also a third professor, named Jarisch. Joe later read in the United States that he had been a member of the committee on the planning of research in concentration camps. He figured that he must have been very lucky to pass all his examinations, having those Nazis as judges. They knew that he was Jewish. He did not see reasons to hide his identity anymore.

He lived in the barracks for foreign students, having to share a cubical with somebody else. At one moment, when he entered his room, he heard a knock at the door, and a young man introduced himself and told him that he was a Pole. Would he like him as his neighbor? "There are many Ukrainians here," he said, "and some of them were perhaps in the service of the Germans." Of course, Joe was delighted to have a Pole as a neighbor.

He was studying, but longed to see me and the baby. I sent him a postcard as if written by Lillian, who was then five months old:

My dearest Daddy:

I have had very many impressions lately. It started with the visit of Uncle Wasserman, who brought me a gift of a beautiful cover for my little bed. It did not happen without scolding Mother. Both Uncle and Aunt yelled at Mother, that she's not raising me properly, that I am the most normal child and best girl, but Mother is spoiling me, carrying me in her arms when I cry, rocking me before sleep. I felt awful, because I saw that Mother is close to crying for the reproof because of me. Besides, what do they know? We have also been visited by Aunt Mina and Uncle Shulim. They enjoyed me very much. Mother left for awhile, and the Aunt kissed me with her fleshy lips at my head bone. In front, this resulted in two fat, bloody spots. Next day, Mother walked like crazy. She said: 'what did they do to the baby? Why was I not careful?' Whoever saw me lamented. All was in order. Then they watched the spot and Mother was astonished. They threw mother unpleasant looks until one aunt suspected that the lipstick might be the responsible culprit. Mother never used the lipstick. When my head had been washed and cleaned up, there was no end to the laughter. The same day, something awful happened. While waiting a long time for my meal, I pulled off the ear of my cat. Now the poor cat walks with his head lowered because it hurts him. Perhaps I'll go with him to the doctor or I'll better wait for you. I kiss your sweet tired eyes.

He was fighting a cold, when a few days later I wrote:

Dear Daddy,

Tell the truth. How long do we have to wait for you? Mother deceived me since Saturday. 'Be polite.' She says, 'Don't cry. Our darling daddy will soon arrive.' And this endlessly continues. Perhaps today, but mother explained to me yesterday that dad is sick, and that we must wait until Thursday, because then he will be completely healthy and will come to us. But, we promise you, we will take good care of you, keep you warm, well fed, put you to sleep, and help you return to normal health. Let only this Thursday come.

Ill luck happened to my cat. I don't know how it happened, but I pulled off his other ear. Mother doesn't permit me to go to strange physicians because she says we have our own. If you could, buy me a large carriage. Thank you for remembering me and for the purchase of the new outfit. If you find two other very nice ones, buy them. It should be large and practical with long pants. This is very important. Also buy a rattle, a dense comb, a brush for clothes, and one for hair. I kiss you strongly, my dear daddy!

Longing,

Your Little Kitten

He seldom had time to leave Innsbruck, but he tried to get into the camp in order to see his sweethearts. There, two sweet heads and two loving hearts waited for him. He bought the baby carriage, brought it to the camp and pushed it with the smiling baby along the winding streets of the town. He liked to stop next to the waterfall, which attracted the eyes of Lillian. If only he could have been closer to his family, he thought! When he returned to Innsbruck, he found the previous letter from Lillian. It was addressed on June 5th, 1947, when Lillian was only two and a half months old. He read:

My Dearest Faraway Daddy:

> I wanted to attach a stamp for four groshes, because I know that children pay half the price everywhere, but Mother attached a second four groshes stamp. Today, I witnessed a sad scene for me: Mother's eyes were wet. In the language of adults, they say someone is crying. The tears remained in her eyes when I ate an apple. As mother explained later, I'm eating an apple with such enthusiasm, with such a lust, and this was the last fruit that she had. Perhaps one can purchase apples in your place because here, unfortunately, one has to walk with one's tongue protruding from want. Yesterday, Mother fell on the bed for the first time. She couldn't endure, poor Mother, while washing my swaddling band. Her eyes were closing against her will, and it was only at that time, ten o'clock in the evening. I wonder, Daddy that you are longing a little for me. Therefore, I confess to you. I keep my head already even. It doesn't rock like a drunkard anymore. Today morning, Mother laid me down on my belly, and I raised my head high, and

Mother was rolling with laughter that I'm able to perform such tricks. I already know how to hold my hands together. I know how to laugh loud. Only the sun is bothering me. The rays are unbearable, and I can't find the right place. Now, it's getting cooler. The sky is getting cloudy. Already the day is getting shorter, and it constantly prepares surprises. I'm very sleepy, and therefore, bye-bye! I kiss you. I kiss your mousy eye, ear, and the moustached mouth.

>Your unforgetful Lillian

As I read this letter, I almost felt the warm head of my daughter and the magnetic wave that pulled me physically close to the only two people of my family that I adored. As soon as I could be able to bring them to Innsbruck, I would solve the separation. But the officer at the Joint would not even listen to me. Later, I found out that he was hoarding food, which had been sent for Jewish students, and had been selling it on the black market.

Soon thereafter came another postcard from Lillian.

My Dearest Daddy:

It has been a long time since I wrote to you, but I always ask mother to add kisses from me to you. Today, I stuck out my tongue and mother bit off a piece. It didn't hurt, but I was mad at mother. I almost lost my eyes because mother drinks them. She says that she's thirsty after each meal. I don't even mention my nose, which she attacks in all directions. This is possible, because I pull mother's hair. According to the principle that hair doesn't grow on a wise head, I pull out handful of her beautiful locks. Today, mother put the kitten in my bed with the doggy. They started to fight, and of course, the doggy won. The poor kitten is lying motionless, and the doggy stuck out his red tongue and is laughing. Every morning when I wake up, I look out of my bed to see if perhaps my sweet Daddy arrived. Mother says in vain that there are only ten more days to wait, and I know that the time will pass swiftly. Mother tries to teach me counting on fingers. She holds one finger until you will come finally. My little baby carriage is already getting too small. I don't have the freedom of movement. I'm constantly getting hurt at its edges. Perhaps, therefore, I'll get a little bed. Then, it will be a paradise. Today, mother ate half a can of sardines. Not bad, isn't it? Darkness descends on the world. Ugly days arrived. It rained heavily, therefore, I'm sitting in the house, and I'm waiting for you, dearest Daddy, until you will pass your examinations. I kiss you so strong that you can't imagine.

> Your Kitten

On July 17th, I sent him a postcard.

My Dear Kitten:

We are not at all sick. We didn't write since Thursday because we were sure you would come Saturday. We are spending the last seven days in heated expectation of you. The flowers prepared for your arrival faded already, and the floor, washed to glittering whiteness, became scratched. Our disposition got sour because we are very sad. One can get crazy from all the gossip around you. One is certain that in a week, one or two months, our camp will be liquidated, and the inhabitants will be segregated according to their arrival in 1945 or in 1946. Do you understand? Do you have the documents from Steyr? We should be translocated to barracks seven kilometers away from Linz. Should I write you that I shivered day and night and I feel like they would already surround the camp with a belt of SS men and weaponry and expose us to new suffering. But all this is nonsense. Important that you pass the examination. We are walking so very proud. If this baby outfit is pink, blue, or green, only these colors, and it is available, buy it for the baby. We kiss you very strong and are waiting impatiently. Marie

It turned out that indeed, the camp in Bad Gastein was to be closed. Joe looked feverishly around Innsbruck for some living quarters for his family. The Jewish camp in Wiesenhof didn't have any accommodations. He had to find temporary lodging for them in the student barracks. He was impressed by the speed with which this was approved. He brought us from Bad Gastein to Innsbruck and we enjoyed togetherness, even though in great discomfort, in a small room in the unheated barracks. There were some students from Romania and Hungary next to us, one of whom had been a former officer in the Iron Guard. Joe was the only Jew in the entire complex on Rechenweg Street. He was identified as the representative of the hated people, and other than official greetings, no closer contact was made with the neighbors.

After a certain amount of prodding, the administration of the camp, Wiesenhof, found lodgings for us. We considered this a Godsend. It was not easy to be admitted to the camp, and it can be assumed that they yielded to pressures by the regional director of the Joint Committee, a Frenchman whom Joe had approached, asking for help. We made new friends. The cross-section of the inhabitants showed a smaller percentage of concentration camp inmates and of partisans than in Bad Gastein. Even here, there was no equality, no democracy as I expected. There was a caste system of those who were in, or close to the administration, and all the others. As in the general population, intellectual values were not at all important. What was important was how much money one had and how good a dealer one was. And this was very unpleasant for us.

Joe frequently walked down the hill from the camp to Solbad Hall to save money for bus fare. And from there, he took a tramway to Innsbruck. The area, though not as picturesque as Bad Gastein, was still very charming. But he had no time to explore the beautiful nature. He had to study and to spare the rest of his time for his family. Only one time did he take the funicular mountain train to Patcherkofer Peak. As he sat in his chair, he silently admired the other carefree passengers who were laughing and feeling merry. The Austrians, together with the Germans, had lost the war, he thought, but look at them now and compare them with us, the only survivors from our entire families, one of few from his city, one of not many of the Jews of Europe, our People.

One afternoon, as we were sitting in the camp in the shade of a spreading tree, I told Joe that I was experiencing symptoms of pregnancy. After waiting a couple of weeks, a physician confirmed my impression.

While most of the camp dwellers knew more or less

where they would like to emigrate, we had no doubts that there was only one place that we would like to go: to Palestine. Nearby the camp was the Bricha, the underground organization that helped Jews get to Palestine. Since Joe was close to finishing his studies, he turned to them for help to emigrate. They excluded that possibility out of hand. They couldn't send a pregnant woman or newborn babies because of the English blockade, which closed all the roads for Jews. And those who were caught on the sea were sent to concentration camps on Cyprus. There was no way to convince them about special situations deserving consideration. While we knew little about other countries, especially about the United States, our desire to go to Palestine was now redirected. The revelation of the heartless attitudes of the democratic Englishmen to the people who had miraculously escaped the gas chambers of the Nazi Germans was the first seed of the idea that the world was not without blemishes, that Christian civilization professed compassion but showed none. As we found out later, while living in the United States, the answer to the question of whether this country also deserves condemnation for its attitude to the European Jews during the Holocaust, is sadly, yes.

In Israel a war of independence was raging against five Arab nations. And Joe felt very guilty for having to spend that critical time in Austria rather than in the ranks of fighting, young Jews. After weeks of extreme tension, there was finally victory, and an independent Jewish state was born after two thousand years of the Diaspora, and after the loss of one-third of the Nation. And for the Rebhuns there was a wonderful celebration one day before the declaration of independence. Joe's professor of obstetrics delivered Lillian's brother, Richard at the University hospital. The delivery was uneventful except that I developed a mild duodenal ulcer and varicose veins. Joe brought the baby and me home. Lillian was being taken care of for some time by a woman from Hungary who had a daughter Lillian's age. Now, we were all four waiting impatiently for Joe's studies to end and for an open door to any country away from the graveyards and criminals of Europe.

On one occasion, we got scared by the appearance of a Soviet commission. The Russian officers tried to get volunteers for repatriation from the countries of Eastern Europe. This ended, fortunately, uneventfully. It was not easy for me to take care of our two babies, separated only by fourteen months, without proper food, diapers, and a washing machine, but I never complained, and I seemed to be very happy. Only in the evening, I would fall exhausted and rest.

Even though England yielded to the pressure of the United Nations and recognized Israel, she continued the blockade, and so there would be no way for us to go to Israel. I found out somehow that there was suddenly an open door for us to emigrate to the United States. Joe told me that he was not able to grasp how I had arranged this, but one time, I left him with the children and found my way to the Joint, and before he knew it, I had placed our names on the list of potential emigrants to the States. It was not easy, and I thank God for my persuasive power as a lawyer. As soon as Joe graduated, he ran home with his diploma, and we started to pack. Within a few days, we were in Bremenhaven, from where we boarded an old Marine ship, General Stuart, bringing us to the Golden Land.

We left behind our dearest people, swept by the cruelty of man into unknown graves, poisoned, and burned, and exposed to brutality before their deaths, to which no behavior of beasts could be compared. We witnessed historical events in comparison with which all past history paled, when technological progress and the fruits of civilization were used to destroy human ethics and morality. There remained only a cry stuck in our throats and a flow of tears. No matter what, with these losses, no happiness, in the true sense of this word, would be known to us, though we anticipated moments, which could be described as happy. A practical approach to life had taken over our emotions. In our most intimate moments, we were constantly reverberating with the experiences of our past, that most recent past in which we had lived. The life in two worlds became a title of Joe's future book, *God and Man in Two Worlds.*

We kept our distance from other immigrants from the old country, not knowing whether they had collaborated with the Nazis or not. We had, of course, no knowledge at that time that some former SS men had got entry visas to the United States before us, and that some of them were deliberately sought out for utilizing their intelligence against the Soviet Union during the Cold War. We only shared our emotions with each other. We soon understood that the drama of our past history was not only rejected by people who lived in the safety and prosperity of the New World, and defended their happiness, but even if they were willing to listen to our report, nobody could even imagine that this had been a reality. Their good life distorted not only comprehension but also all reasoning.

Joe decided, however, with all his strength, to tell the story no matter what. He decided to speak up against evil because he saw that the explosion of technology without morality was not going to bring mankind any salvation. As a survivor of the greatest tragedy that ever befell any group of people, in spite of his suffering, facing untold experiences of human evil on a daily basis, he felt an obligation to describe this evil to protect the species from a repetition of this on a larger scale. He realized that, without morality, the very technological explosion could be utilized for destructive goals instead of the bettering of mankind. At that time, the United States and Russia grabbed and protected Nazi scientists to use their knowledge for future wars with each other.

Until Martin Luther King's time, the struggle for civil rights in this country couldn't convince him that ours is a true democracy. Although there was no comparison with the Holocaust, it was very disturbing for a man who believed in absolute social justice. He was later moved by a black woman who introduced herself years later in a spa and said that she was privileged to meet him after she had read his book about the Jewish tragedy in Europe. "What should we talk," she said, "when we compare our suffering with yours? It was indeed my privilege to meet you." We were both condemned, she by the color of her skin, and we for our belief, even though we both were productive citizens with love of our countries. It took a small group headed by individuals like Hitler or Stalin, to galvanize an entire nation to build gas chambers and the gulag.

I was optimistic about the future, and Joe was the one who was cautious and pessimistic. I trusted people, while he always expected a repetition of our tragedy, which might affect any group of people, as long as they didn't learn from our history.

We landed in the Bronx, where we lived in a room of an apartment of a sweet Jewish widow by the name of Rubinfeld. Joe got a job as an intern shortly thereafter at Barnert Memorial Hospital in Patterson, New Jersey for a salary of seventy dollars a month. In order to help him, I got a job in a carpet factory. I rushed there in the morning after putting the children in a preschool. Richard had to be watched very closely. At the age of two-and-a-half he would suddenly run into the middle of the avenue and try to stop the traffic. Now, Joe had a chance to visit his family more often than when we had lived in Austria. The distance was not far, and the bus service was excellent. We discovered the American opium: television. We used it primarily when the children were around.

Joe headed for the emergency room when another intern by the name of Klima handed him a newspaper with his name and an article describing how he had brought a pregnant patient in by ambulance and had delivered her baby while stepping out of the ambulance. Overnight, he became a local celebrity. He brought the newspaper to me, and I proudly put my arms around his neck and kissed my hero. He assisted in the operating room, and he saw the first lobotomies performed by Dr. Freeman. Here, he was also exposed to direct care of patients, and here he started to love them. Still, he could not share his daily emotions with me. He was on call every second night, and the work day was ten to twelve hours, with daily rounds, consultations, and writing histories and progress notes.

We watched the news on television and with great trepidation we followed the political news: the gathering clouds over Israel and the developing Cold War between the United States and the Soviet Union. There were indicators of a possible conflict in either theater. We had our reservations as to the factual and impartial press releases, however. Because of our past experience we were pessimistic that peace would prevail in spite of the superiority of the weapons that the United States had.

By the end of the year, having a good record, Joe started to think about a medical residency. He sought advice from the men who wanted to support his application in New York hospitals in which they were attending physicians. They sometimes took him there to the clinicopathological seminars. He remembered how they brought him one time to Atlantic City and bought him lunch. After the meal, all were served lemons with their napkins to clean their hands. The doctors, knowing that he came from Europe and that he was not accustomed to that luxury, signaled each other with elbows, smiling and wondering what he would do—eat the lemon or use it for washing his hands. He noticed their conspiracy, and he chose to do none of the above. They then had a good laugh. They brought him to the car with arms linked, and they drove back to Patterson.

Joe got several interesting offers, but he chose the Cornell University infirmary and Tompkins County Hospital in Ithaca, New York. In the meantime, he found my stepbrother, Stas Simon, who lived with his wife, a former nurse, and a son in Nutley, New Jersey. He had come here just before the war broke out, to see the World's Fair, and while serving in the army, took part in the Battle of the Bulge. Afterward, he became a successful architect. We accepted his offer to share his house with me and the children. We spent six weeks there until Joe found an apartment in Ithaca. Stas asked details about the family and how they had perished, but Joe saw he could not perceive the enormity of the suffering and losses. When he described some of the dramatic acts during the Holocaust with a smile, Stas asked him how he could smile while telling such gruesome stories. Joe answered him, if one cannot cry anymore, one laughs.

At that point, I started to help out again. I got a job at Woolworth's in Ithaca, and while the children were in preschool, I supplemented Joe's meager salary. We now lived together, and I was very happy about this course of events. On Sundays, except when Joe was on duty, we made picnics on the shore of Lake Cayuga. We went to Cornell University or we took a walk downtown. Here Joe also started to do a research project with one of the professors at the veterinary school on rumen factor. The scenic beauty of the local hills reminded him somewhat of his hometown, Przemysl, and the waterfalls reminded us of Bad Gastein.

The attending physicians were very cordial and caring. One of the residents, Bob Lichtenstein, became our lifelong friend. Joe still remembers three patients. One was a girl in her late teens with dermatomyositis. Another, a president of the American Chemical Society, was a heavy drinker. He drunk heavily only about three months every year, and the chief of medicine took personal care of sobering him up. The third patient was responsible for Joe's choosing allergy as a subspecialty. At admission, she had obvious symptoms of asthma. She was admitted with the diagnosis of cerebral accident with partial paralysis. Because of her acute asthma, Joe administered an injection of adrenaline, which not only alleviated the wheezing, but also relieved the symptoms of the cerebral accident. She started to talk immediately and her paralysis disappeared. She told him that this time, her 'stroke' was more severe, but she always had it in past years on the Fourth of July, when the family gathered and when she served pork, which she otherwise never ate. This became an intriguing point and he immediately started to consult books. She soon went home with the diagnosis of allergy to pork, and a warning to avoid this meat in the future. He remained with the desire to more deeply explore the fascinating field of allergy.

When his residency was about to end, he started to write applications for fellowships or residency programs in allergy. He was invited to serve as a fellow at Northwestern University under the tutorship of Professor Sam Feinberg, who became not only his teacher but a lifelong friend. He combined clinical work with laboratory research, which eventually ended in 1954 with a postdoctorate Master's degree in science and with several publications. During the examinations, the department Head of Medicine, Arthur Caldwell, who otherwise liked Joe, disagreed with his answer to a question in immunology, but he was immediately corrected by Feinberg and the third member of the examining committee. Joe immediately became an instructor in medicine and a medical researcher with a promise to take over control of the laboratory, which had been until then under the leadership of Joe's immediate superior and friend, Doctor Malkiel.

Independently from his work in the allergy department, Joe participated in some independent research with the head of the Department of Biochemistry, Professor Albert Zeller. We spent a number of weekends visiting both with the Zellers and Feinbergs. Zeller was the discoverer of the diamine-oxidase enzyme, responsible for histamine degradation, and enjoyed the high regard of his colleagues. He was Swiss and was very broad-minded and very humble. When he called Joe at home several times, I had difficulty in understanding his heavy accent. Yet he corrected numerous papers published by his students and coworkers.

As a result of a non-sterile procedure in a dental office, I developed serum hepatitis. I was very sick and I was hospitalized at the Passavant University Hospital, where I was a neighbor of a famous politician: in the room next to mine was Adlai Stevenson.

Just before that illness our son, Donald, was born in June of 1953. At his birth, the obstetrician came late, and the attending nurse tried to convince me to behave very calmly and she tried to push the baby back by pressing the already engaged head. The doctor apologized and delivered the baby who, according to Joe, looked more at the time like Mussolini rather than he or I. We were immensely happy with this first true American in our family.

We felt more secure, even though my salary of two hundred and fifty dollars a month did not change. Joe bought our first car, a Chevrolet, which we now used instead of public transportation. The only exception was Joe's traveling to Gary, Indiana, where he worked for an allergist attending the allergy clinic, Simon Rubin. The extra money augmented our living standard, and he had planned a permanent academic career and the opening of his office in Hammond, Indiana. I supported him, and emotionally we were very happy in spite of the fact that we were relatively poor people.

Joe received also at the time an invitation from Professor Althausen, the Head of the Department of Medicine at the University of California in San Francisco to take over the Allergy Department with a temporary rank of Assistant Professor and with an annual salary of five thousand dollars plus bonuses, which was great for the time. This letter arrived just prior to Joe's opening an office in Hammond, Indiana. He had already printed announcements about opening the office, and he received some phone calls from doctors who needed an allergist to consult in their practices.

Then, suddenly, he received an order for active reserve duty in the army. Since this was the time of the still raging Korean War, we were afraid of separation again. He might be sent to Korea or Germany. But soon, he was notified that the army had only three allergists, and that the one in San Francisco, Captain Raymer, had just finished his tour of duty, and that he was being assigned to replace him as the chief of the allergy clinic and assistant chief of the outpatient department. I blossomed for the next few days, saying that we couldn't have dreamed of a better assignment. Joe had to first go through basic training in Fort San Houston, Texas, where they kept him for only eighteen days. He learned how to handle a gun, which he already knew, how to salute when you pass a car of a general, and how to recognize ranks. San Francisco saw him soon, and here he was greeted by General Fancher and Colonel Bill Hollifield, both physicians. "Captain Rebhun, we are delighted to have you here," said the General and shook his hand. Bill Hollifield became one of Joe's best friends in the States. He was overwhelmed with their warmth and friendship. Thus started his tour of duty of almost three years, happy years in the United States Army. Fridays, after work, he had to join the General and Bill for the happy hour, a new discovery for a man who had not drunk alcohol since he was made drunk by his Russian superior in 1941.

What followed was above all expectations for Joe, who had almost been killed only twelve years before by the Nazis after he jumped off the transport to Auschwitz, and for me, who was at the same time at the bottom of the abyss. He was full of joy when he picked me up from the airport, with the older two children and sweet, little Donny, only two years old. We were finally together, and my silent prayer was that we would always stay like this. We moved to a rented house at 106 Edna Street. He was going to work in the morning and coming back home to his family, where he could remove his uniform and be a civilian husband and daddy.

His office was next to Bill Hollifield's, across the hall from the head of the hospital, General Fancher, and of the commanding officer of the base, Colonel Thomas Sheen. He couldn't free himself from invitations to the happy hour on Fridays, but he got used to it and he was very careful coming back home. As the Zellers and the Feinbergs had done before, now the Hollifields began inviting us to visit with them on weekends. Bill listened to Joe's past history and told him his. He was born in the mountain regions of Virginia. He had never seen nor had he ever known a Jew. His mother used to tell him stories about Jews having well-hidden horns. While in college, he always followed Jewish students to the bathroom to discover where they hide their horns. Until now, however, he had had no luck to find out, and his best friend became a Jewish doctor of dermatology, a professor at Stanford, and now Joe became his second friend. He always shook his hands with a deep, warm look in his eyes. They ate lunch together, and Joe replaced him during his occasional absence in the office. Although he was an allergist by training, as Joe was, he did not step into the allergy clinic, leaving its control entirely to Joe. His teacher was known in the specialty, Professor Oscar Swineford. Joe loved the Army life immensely, particularly, as he frequently repeated, considering that it was only twelve years since he was able to make his way from his nightmare and the jump from the transport to Auschwitz to his present rank of a captain in the U.S Army.

We got in touch with old acquaintances in San Francisco, with the Lichtensteins, whom Joe had befriended in Ithaca, New York, and with the Shelubs, whom we accidentally discovered. After many years, we renewed our friendship. Bob was now working for Kaiser Permanente as an allergist and lived in Oakland, and the Shelubs, whom we had not seen since we left BadGastein, lived in San Francisco. We met on weekends for walks and dinners.

Joe made loose contacts with a local synagogue, and he frequently communicated with the rabbi assigned to the base. He had to find a quorum twice a year to say the prayer for the departed, on the death anniversaries of his father and mother. There was a Passover Seder organized for the military personnel, and we celebrated the High Holidays. Otherwise, there was no involvement in Jewish communal life.

I was busy with the Girl Scouts and also with the Boy Scouts, as soon as Richard and Lillian grew up. Joe's firm social position gave me peace of mind, calmness and satisfaction. Joe volunteered his work as a physician to the Boy Scout camp Royaneh, with over five hundred boys and scoutmasters when the great Asian influenza epidemic broke out in 1957. He was busy for several days and nights since almost the entire camp caught the illness, including our children, who were with him.

It was getting close to his discharge from the Army, and I decided that we were better off remaining in California than going back to his practice and teaching in Chicago. Joe explored the situation by going south, and he found Pomona Valley with the penetrating smell at that time of orange trees, with blue skies in the foothills of Mt.

Baldy. He made his choice, and we made our home there.

Bill Hollifield coughed more and more. This did not prevent his smoking like a chimney, one cigarette after another. Not long thereafter, we received a letter from Kay Hollifield that her husband, and Joe's friend Bill, had died.

In order to supplement our income, since he could not make enough money in the beginning as a new allergist in the community, which didn't know exactly what an allergist was, Joe worked as an internist at Pacific State Hospital for several months and also for a private medical group. He was the only allergist between Los Angeles and Nevada, except for an older allergist in Riverside.

I helped Joe in the office, but eventually I was able stay home after Joe got a secretary.

We started to build our new home in an area, which was covered with orange orchards, which exuded an intoxicating aroma in the spring. With sorrow, we had to remove the trees from our property. Skies were seemingly always blue, the air fresh, and there was at that time still no smog, which appeared only three years later. The only air pollution during the winter was caused by the smudging of the trees. After we bought our furniture and settled in our house with a view of Mt. Baldy, we were overwhelmed by the present good life, relatively, so shortly after the horrible hell we had experienced in Europe. Joe's attention could not be diverted from the intensity of that past even for a day, and occasionally, he shared his thoughts with me, who seldom initiated those conversations, despite the fact that I had more reasons than Joe, according to him, to go back in my memory since I suffered much in the camps.

Our children were growing up in fabulous surroundings. Joe was giving me all the credit for their upbringing. He helped me. He sees from the perspective of time that he was so obsessed with the Holocaust, having devoted so much time to that subject, that he probably neglected the present world for the one which he had lost. I was a bond in the glue of the two worlds in which he existed, and an inspiration to live in reality. He needed my serene companionship, he said, and enthusiasm for children and exultation for life.

We constantly dreamed about visiting Israel. While in the Army, we took short trips to Nevada, to the Grand Canyon, to the Canadian borders, but the visit abroad was just a dream. One time, while wading in the pool in Las Vegas, I suddenly lost my footing and I started to drown. Fortunately, Joe was next to me and pulled me out. I was awfully scared. This was the second time that I was saved in the water. Before the war I was rescued by a swimmer from the waters of the Vistula River in Warsaw. We visited Hawaii, and finally, in 1960, we could financially afford to undertake the trip to Israel.

Even though we made a number of of trips to Israel later on, that first excursion became the most memorable, symbolizing a bridge with all the holiness and dearness of the past. Trying to hide my deep emotions, we finally arrived there. We visited the only surviving branch of the family, Joe's mother's sister, Mirta Chary, who had the chance to run away from Munich, Germany in 1933. She was a spry woman, who walked every day of the year to swim in the Mediterranean Sea. She looked like Joe's mother and reminded him so much of the woman who gave him life and whom he adored over everything else. Her husband Bernard and her son in law were German Jews and spoke German with us. We stayed in the house of Lotte, their daughter, who had two lovely daughters, Gila and Ariela. Joe's cousin, Joseph Chary, Lotte's brother, was a professor of economics and a retired army major. We accepted his offer to be our guide in exploring the Holy Land. He knew the small country as well as his own back yard in Zahala, where he lived. This was an educational excursion that left us with unforgettable memories. We received a geography lesson of both ancient and current history, and relived Joseph's report of how he himself had helped to build and defend the country. Joe's Aunt regretted that we had not brought the children with us. She would have liked to see them so very much. Instead, she had to be satisfied with old pictures of the smiling Lillian, Richard, and little Donny.

We also found my uncle and cousins, the only survivors of my family. They had immigrated to Palestine before World War II. My uncle, Eliezer Cygelman, was a Talmud-educated Jew, an author of a book, a copy of which he gave us as a gift. He and my mother, Regina were two of seven children of Noach Cygelman. They all perished with their families during the Holocaust. Eliezer had a bookstore in Haifa. There, his son, Menachem Cygelman, also worked. The son was divorced and had two wonderful children. He got our admiration for his physical fitness. He ran, hiked, and swam in the Mediterranean.

During future visits to Israel, we stayed at his sister's house on Montefiore Street in Haifa.

In spite of my unpleasant experience with the paternal line of the family during the war, I always was proud of my unknown relatives. Two of my uncles were professors of mathematics at the university in Moscow and a third uncle lived in Harbin, China, married to a non-Jewish woman.

We fell in love with Haifa. This was for us like the Israeli San Francisco, an enchanted spot, especially at sunrise and sunset. The brightness of the rays were reflected in the mild waves of the bay and the glitter of the golden dome of the Baha'i Temple, where the prayers of the believers and the crescent of the blue skies touched the horizon of the hills on the opposite side of the bay of the Mediterranean Sea. Haifa was for us a natural expression of beauty and holiness, surpassed only by Jerusalem.

When my cousin, who was a lawyer, told us that I had

inherited property in Petach Tikwa from another departed uncle by the name of Barkai, Joe decided without hesitation to donate the money from the sale of that property to the Technion Medical School. The Medical School had just been organized by Professor David Ehrlik, and Joe struck up a friendship with this man immediately. We became founders and guardians of the Technion. A much greater joy of accomplishment was given to Joe with his organization of the allergy clinic a few years later. The material support didn't mean as much as seeing a place, which he had helped to create, bustling with the activity of daily help to allergy sufferers from the entire area.

After the Holocaust, Israel's development was understood by us to be a demonstration of historical justice for a people who have the same right to live freely as any other nation.

After the return from Israel, Joe received a letter from Rabbi Robinson, who inquired about his knowledge of Schwammberger, the German head of the ghetto in Joe's hometown, who supposedly had been caught by the Western authorities with eight sacks of gold, pearls, and other jewelry, which he was supposed to turn over to the German authorities. Instead, he had stolen it from them. Therefore, years later, when the presiding judge asked Joe during the court procedure against Schwammberger what was his opinion about the man against whom he testified, since he had seen him killing several Jews in ghetto B, where he lived, he did not call him a killer, because killing Jews was, at that time, a legal procedure ordered by the government, but he called him a thief, because he was stealing Jewish jewelry from his own Führer, whom he served. Schwammberger, however, was at the time able to escape to South America, from where he was eventually extradited to Germany.

CHAPTER TWENTY-TWO

OUR HOME

Living in Claremont was associated with social importance since professional people and college professors lived there, and our little town was known as a cultural area. The people who lived in downtown Pomona often snubbed us as their only way of getting even. People who lived in Claremont were very often overcharged for services by workers who did home repairs. When a high school team would come to play and compete with our high school kids, dirty slogans and abusive language would appear. Yet, all people in Pomona envied us, the foothill dwellers, and wouldn't have minded themselves or their children to live with us. There were community activities which brought both groups of the population together very closely and a friendly relationships finally developed.

Spring brought with it a wave of heat and also the smell of jasmine and orange blossoms. Mother Earth, covered with fresh grasses, caused many noses to get stuffed, and hay fever sufferers swallowed antihistamines to get relief. Nose blowing here and there found an echo in a loud, diffuse sneeze.

Originally, we got together more often with local physicians, but soon, an incident in the social life of the community caused our restraint. One town affair remained memorable. Around the well-lit pool at the party of physicians, people gathered under trees and were hidden in the shadows of a house and held glasses of alcohol in their hands. Occasionally, the darkness was brightened by a match. The hum of voices would die out for a moment, interrupted occasionally by laughter or a loud voice. From the darkness of the yard, one could better see the silhouettes of the people and sparkling stars. There was no sign of a wind. The water, night, warmth, smells, alcohol, and the closeness of both sexes were conducive to sin. As a result of this party, there was wife swapping, and what struck the community like a comical thunder was that five respectable couples split and swapped partners. What was the real cause of this small epidemic, I wouldn't like to guess, perhaps a fashion that they liked to follow. Since that happened, we limited our attendance at parties and happy hours.

When I stopped working in the office, Joe usually called me from the office at least once or twice during the day to find out how I was doing and how the children were.

Joe did not like any surgery unless it was unavoidable. Therefore, he opposed my decision to strip my veins, which really had not bothered me and only created a cosmetic problem. I enjoyed good health. One time, I was even able to climb to the top of Mt. Baldy with Joe. I did not like the varicose veins that I had acquired during pregnancy. He finally gave in to my nagging, and this was a fatal decision. My surgery was performed by a friend, who was also Joe's patient. He asked Joe to assist him during the surgery. Immediately after surgery, I developed a massive pulmonary embolism, which almost killed me. The treatment of heparin injections for almost a year was followed by oral anticoagulants. I almost died as a result of this avoidable surgery, and after that I developed changes in my lungs, which contributed to my illness over a period of years.

Now we realized our vulnerability. We tried to verbalize our deep feelings to each other.

CHAPTER TWENTY-THREE

My Loss

Her sweet smile, which she displayed most of the time, led me not to understand how she could muster and control her painful past with so much dignity? Her soft, curly hair flowing like an areola around her radiating face, was comforting and healing after my severe psychological traumas of the Holocaust. She took up a different appearance only during that period of time when she did not enjoy good health.

She brought peace to my soul. With the flow of generations, there is a small wave of goodness that is unforgettable. This was Marie. She was not only my beloved partner, but the breath of our common history and experience. She loved the world and couldn't even hate her enemies. She was always a loyal wife, leaving serious decisions for me. In the dusk of our life, we had no doubts about each other's friendship and fidelity. There was always the harmony of trust. She said: "You are my best friend," and she meant it. During her illness, I cuddled her and kissed her blue eyes, and she would say: "How wonderful you are!" And this sentence still soothes me. Her kindness had not changed with the many years that we lived together. We could not understand the dissonance and separations of other families. She would feel so innocent when she brought her unwrinkled face next to mine and I still feel her warmth around me and in me. The torment after her loss is visceral. My thoughts fly to her day and night.

She spent the last days of her life in a peaceful, childlike concentration of deep sleep. She kept her eyes closed and did not respond to painful stimuli or injection. She only raised her arms occasionally to enlarge the space of her thoracic cavity. She obviously had great difficulty breathing. She seemed to concentrate on the separation from life. Doped with medication, she rarely betrayed the devastating cardiac pain that she had on admission to the hospital and only her abdomen moved spasmodically at times.

The love that she had for her children and grandchildren radiated until the very end before it disappeared in a world of shadows. How did I react immediately after her loss? It was an unusual void and pain. The pain produced tears and caused me to choke up. It changed my nature to a point that I could not even control my voice during my public speaking. This was a magnetic attraction of two souls, of two partners who became one. After she was gone, it was like tearing one body apart and dying.

When the smell of trees and flowers reached my nostrils again with the warm breeze of the spring, it became a reminder of the soft feeling of her neck, a part of gentleness and dignity with which she radiated. She talked to me with her presence, even when she kept silent, when her eyes turned to me, caring and pulling stronger than a thousand magnets, even when she was immobile, afraid of death devouring her body. I have lately focused all my attention on her, not on her sick body, but on who she was and how she brought riches to my life, riches of goodness and godliness.

Having each other and having unlimited trust in each other partially replaced our dark, commonly shared past:

the loss of our families and of our people. The family that we built was an expression of self-preservation, a grasping for life, for meaning, for defiance of evil. I verbalized this more often than she did, but we both did it consciously. If I could turn back time, I would like to express to Marie some more of my thankfulness for being with me and complementing my spirit.

We rarely had a disagreement, which is unavoidable in a period of fifty-four years, but if we did, she never held this against me. In her sweetness, she repeated that she had nobody to protect her but me, her best friend. The fact that she was a woman who suffered so much in her life and still showed so much love and nobility, was one of the main reasons why our marriage enjoyed longevity and harmony.

CHAPTER TWENTY-FOUR

ALONE

I was not given the opportunity to kiss my mother on her deathbed, as I did Marie. I could not ask my mother's forgiveness and express my eternal love. Both these two women became confluent in my emotions, and they were the object of one feeling. Their image became the same, and my outpouring of love for them also became confluent in one deep emotion, in one wave. My memory brings their image in front of me very frequently. Both women lived for their families. Both loved their people and children. They had, however, some differences.

My mother was mystically religious, fearing God, and loving mankind. Marie was more educated in Judaism than my mother, but her religious background was so much poorer than Mother's. Both women loved me immensely and trusted me. I was with both of them almost until that last moment of their lives. Mother's figure jumping out of the train to Auschwitz is still in front of me, vivid, and it became etched in my memory forever. The last kiss I gave Marie in the open coffin is also eternal. There was a trusting and otherworldly value in this gesture. I pray that these forms of last departure stay with me forever.

Marie's smooth skin expressed a lasting act of unity, and of love that even death could not part. She was the symbol of and the thread linking me to the Holocaust. The tragic history and the symbol merged together and formed a holiness of tradition, which cannot die as long as I live. Marie's sweetness and care, and the love for my mother, is felt simultaneously while I am sitting down, while I am lying down, and while I am getting up, with my morning and evening prayer, whenever I raise my eyes to God. It chokes me up, even at my age.

The love of these two women with their gentle souls permeates me and becomes a part of me. I got the opportunity to follow the Jewish custom of mourning for seven days, sitting Shiva, following the death of Marie. I had no similar chance to sit Shiva for my mother and for my father, for all other members of my family, or after my people perished during the Holocaust.

Marie became a symbol for me. In spite of my feeling of loss for those who perished, I had Marie as some compensation, as the living symbol of the Holocaust, until I also lost her. Does death bring us only loss, night, and darkness or is it a return to the original existence, as the rabbis and other clergymen would like us to believe? A rabbi said: "You have to divorce yourself from a rational, scientific approach in order to enter the world of spirituality." I don't yet know how to do it. But I agree with him, that in need of finding inner peace, it is possible that death is not the end of our existence. I shall try.

After a period of devastation, emptiness, and feeling as low as the grave in which Marie rests, a new thought is very gradually rising within me: to do all I can for her, to anticipate what she would have liked me to do, until I stop breathing and become her geographical neighbor at Hillside Cemetery.

I tried to understand why my children could not experience the same devastating loss of Marie as I. And now, I believe I understand. They lost their mother, a very painful experience. I lost a friend, a lover, but most importantly, I lost a symbol of the entire European Jewry annihilated during the Holocaust. They are young, they are Americans, and they are influenced by the material world more than I ever was. They are not sensitized by previous losses. When I look in the mirror, I see a man with a gray beard, which grew during the time since I lost Marie, and which brings out a similarity with my father, who was shot by the Nazis in 1942. This familiarity with the past lights up the dismal loneliness and gives me some comfort. I live in two worlds almost with equal intensity, in the present real one and in the past, the lost one.

I don't feel punished more than anybody else, since everybody will eventually enter the world of Marie. Her body will not suffer anymore. I wish that the rest of my family during the Holocaust left life with Marie's dignity. Her body finally broke down, after suffering in twelve camps and enduring many years of illness, but her spirit resisted, and she retained her goodness and gentleness.

When I lost my father and mother and the rest of my family and my people, I was living under unusual stress. I was fighting for life every second. Perhaps the loss of a peaceful sense of safety is felt stronger, when one feels more comfortable.

After she passed away, I formulated questions in my mind as others had done before me: if the existence of the soul depends on the life of the body, is it worthwhile to despair after a loss of the body? Sooner or later, we also will turn into some simple organic chemicals. We will not need anything, even such an unlimited love as I feel for Marie. If the soul exists, beyond material existence, beyond the perishable body, then we'll meet again.

Marie's agonizing struggle with death ended with her defeat, or who knows? Perhaps her struggle ended with liberation from physical suffering. Her body and character always projected gentleness and caring. As long as she was enjoying health, she was helping others, and this endeared her to her family and all her friends.

A part of me was gone with Marie's departure. To raise me from my deep loss and depression, my children suggested a trip to the Holy Land, which we visited together numerous times and which was the uniting center of our common love. I was persuaded and I went with my son Richard and his friend Christina to see the land that Marie and I dreamed to see together once more, to find consolation and to follow the steps of our great teachers, philosophers and martyrs. I also wanted to see the latest demographic changes in the country.

From Heathrow, we took a plane to Tel-Aviv, and left London behind, which was cloudy and morose. In Tel-Aviv, we stayed next to the beach. We came during the red sundown, which was absolutely astonishing. In the morning, we walked along the beach, when the moon and the sun were still on the opposite side of the firmament. People were already wading in the Mediterranean. Some of them were running, and they were playing the game named 'matka.'

We stopped in a hotel and talked with a woman who was from Rumania. She told us that two of her sons, after the army service, went back to Bucharest, one to study medicine, and the other, veterinary medicine. She had been living in the country for ten years, and she felt very happy.

I called my friend from my hometown, Przemysl, Joseph Goren, and we made a date for the next day. The Mediterranean Sea, in the meantime, had turned greenish blue on the horizon, calm, with only a few mild waves hitting the shore. The city homes look like a Lego play. It was nothing that would attract me to this city in the Biblical or historical sense. It is a new Western city. There was nothing to remind me of the Canaanites or other people, who had lived here before Joshua conquered this land.

The morning walk was stimulating. As I walked, I observed the features of the people who were passing me on the streets. There were only a few characters whom I would classify as looking Jewish. Some had Russian features, while others bore the features of oriental Jews. The inscriptions on the stores were in Russian and Hebrew. I asked myself: what identifies those people as belonging to one nation? I immediately saw a similarity with the Melting Pot of the United States. People from all over the world came here. They are not a part of the nation yet, but eventually they will melt into a body, which is represented by a common culture and, perhaps, common religion. Right now, they are many people who are Greek Orthodox, and there are, of course, those believing in Islam, and many Christians who lived here before the last wave of immigration.

We stopped for a coffee in a restaurant. The woman who served us was speaking Russian. She was born in Leningrad. Indeed, if not for knowing that I was in Tel-Aviv, looking at the faces and listening to the Russian spoken around, I would have had the impression that I am in Russia.

There is a constant traffic and noise on Ben Yehuda Street during the day, which slightly dissipates at night. We were walking along the shore of the Mediterranean, and there were breakwaters prepared for the comfort of bathers. They protruded their black surfaces contrasting with the lights of the sky and sea. The walk is named the Shlomo Lahat promenade. The clouds with their silvery edges dispersed and the half moon appeared again, and there was another day in Tel-Aviv. The rays of the sun look over the crowns of yellow palms, and my longing for my wife persists and it is becoming more intense with the onset of the night. Again, tears are pressing against my tear ducts, and Marie's calling comes to me without the closeness of her warm body.

My visit to the museum of The Diaspora was enriching. We saw a number of young people who spoke Russian. I asked them in Russian if they are Jewish. They answered affirmatively. But I did not hear from them even one Hebrew word. I was told that some of them were not Jewish, but that they had come to Israel because it is the land of opportunity. They work about five hours a day on the kibbutz, and are allowed to use the rest of the times as they please.

The Museum watchman told me that some of the Russian immigrants were able to falsify their documents and pretend to be Jewish. What is it that makes this country of immigrants different from other countries, to call it a Jewish state? Not necessarily the present population. It gathers in people from all over the world, some of whom are not Jews; some of them are not believers in Judaism. Yet, I see here a pioneering spirit, which is not as great as in the past, but still detected when you are speaking with the older citizens. Contained within this small nation is the historical mystery of the country, the tradition to plant a new life on the graves of the past, the continuation of the people who are strongly affected by the Holocaust, and a belief in the Jewish credo of construction in place of destruction.

We left Tel-Aviv and went south, crossing the Judean Desert. And here, I recalled Bishop Pike, who perished here. His son attended the same class with my son, Richard.

The undulating sand hills looked so different than our southern Californian deserts. We came to the biblical city of Jericho, which is supposed to be ten thousand years old, and the oldest city with walls, which date back to at least 2200 BC. Here, we saw American, German, Danish, and even Japanese tourists.

We slowly descended to the Dead Sea, where the indicating sign was 394 meters below sea level. We passed and visited Qumran, where the caves were discovered with the Dead Sea Scrolls, the waving hills of the Judean Desert and we came to the shores of the Dead Sea. The table of the water was very calm and only tiny, hardly detectable waves, caused by the wind, could be seen. There was a reflection of the sunny and blue sky in the grayish-blue water. On the other side, we saw the mountains of Jordan, with their upper edges cut almost like with a ruler, forming an even line. There was one solitary tree that told us that even here, where nothing else grows, and where there are no animals, life is possible.

After a day on the Dead Sea we went south and we saw Masada on our right side. I had climbed it twice before, once with Marie and once at the time when I was attending a course of modern Hebrew, the Ulpan. It is miraculous how the Romans were able to bring their catapults and other machines to conquer this fortress. It's just unbelievable. But, it is also unbelievable that the mighty Roman Empire has not been in existence for almost sixteen centuries.

The Dead Sea turns a turquoise color with different shades of green. Hundreds of small hills have flattened heads like mud-pies, as if a man had flattened their heads with a cake knife. Also, the beige walls of the mountains look as if they had been prepared by a man and painted by a man. Above the other side of the sea is the setting sun, which is reflected in the water. A delicate zephyr cools the face. The flattened hills and the rocks look like they were frozen at the time of creation. Finally, shadows descend on this atrium to paradise.

Well, it comes to mind the question asked by some Jews: why didn't Moses lead the Jews to Saudi Arabia rather than lead them through this tortuous way of living and experiencing the hardship of the desert? When you are here, I believe that the answer is simple. This experience teaches you that instead of an oil-rich country, Moses gave the Jews something more valuable than oil: the Ten Commandments, the basis of human morality.

We pass Sodom, the place where God's wrath was experienced by people who were immoral. It is questionable if their immorality was even close to the immorality that I experienced during the Second World War. Since my liberation, I have been looking backwards like Lot's wife, everyday, and if dwelling in the past is punishable, I should have been crystallized by now. Well, there was a stony structure with the inscription, 'Lot's wife.' I winked at her, and I waved my hand, but she didn't wave back to me. The evil is sometimes so great that you are not supposed to look back. But how can you create tomorrow without remembering and evaluating yesterday?

The area looked as if it could have been sunk during the formation of our planet.

We were passing a road that goes only a few yards away from the Jordan border. Only sagebrush grows here. There were no birds or wild animals. This is a real desert. There was a tiny, fine line of clouds in the sky, and one wonders if this is indeed the act of the Creator. It almost looks like a computer-generated graphic. Finally, we saw the first birds: a swallow and an ostrich.

We passed the Kibbutz Yotvata, the same name as the restaurant in Tel-Aviv where we ate a few days before. On the side of the road was an aqueduct. On the Jordanian side some settlements were visible. Akaba was very close. There was a border check, and we came through Eilot to Eilat. We were here with Marie in 1960, when it was a very small community. Now, it had grown to become a most beautiful resort town with magnificent hotels. Here, the desert turned to life, like Marie turned her life from the Death March to life with me. I did not recognize the city. I was here once with Marie and once by myself. What a difference! It is a resort with many modern hotels.

Marie remains close to me with her spirit and she lives in me. She looks through my eyes at this land and approves of my judgment as she did before. She says, "We will meet again," as I close my eyes for the night, praying for her and for my parents, who never heard of Eilat or of the independent Israel.

The next day we left Eilat and went to Jordan. On the Israeli side, all the border crossing formalities took a matter of minutes. The passport procedures on the Jordanian side of the border lasted for hours. The excuse was that the computer had malfunctioned. To cross the border, we paid two hundred dollars for the three of us. We started to move north toward Petra. We passed the phosphate excavations, and a train carrying the precious mineral. There was an occasional green patch. The sky was blue again, and there were a few clouds gathering on the horizon. We passed the road to Wadi Rum and compared the area with Monument Valley in Utah. From far away, the mountains looked like chiseled castles or stacks of hay. We were passing some Arab villages. There was no other vehicle on the road and sometimes we saw a camel. Somebody was working in the field. Finally, we saw Bedouins with flocks of sheep, a truck, a car, and man-made stone signs. We passed Prince Hassan's house, and we had a far view of the mountains of Petra, similar in beauty to the Grand Canyon, except so different. The driver showed us a peak, Jebel Aaron, where Jesus, according to one of the versions, is supposed to have been baptized. The area looked as if it might have been frozen in time, just after creation. We passed Tayba village, the Petra View Hotel, and admired the different colors, similar to those of the Painted Desert in Arizona.

Finally, we came to Wadi Musa Village, with stone walls retaining the sidewalks. Without comments about the wonderful nature and man-made carvings, which are stunning, we entered the Forum hotel. "Marie, you see Petra through my eyes. This is the ancient Nabatean metropolis-necropolis. The spirits of those departed here are not better off than those at Hillside cemetery where your body lies, and where I'll join you."

My father and mother, the rest of my family, and most of the Jews I had known before the war, are buried in Poland. They have one graveyard, and that is Poland itself. There are no monuments. There are hardly any ashes to be detected, but all of these people, nevertheless, live in my heart and I commune with them daily.

Petra demonstrates how man's genius can create an eternal monument using God's gift, nature, and ingenuity. With their limited means of technology, these men who lived here left proof for posterity that human effort could build monasteries and graves in these rocks.

Here, one can find visitors from many countries. We listened to the religious songs of a group of Catholics accompanied by their clergymen from Italy. This is a place to commune with God, no matter what one's religion is. Our hotel was very comfortable. A few birds were sitting on the parapet of the pool, while other were flying over it and dipping their beaks into the surface. The food was excellent. The Bedouins are exceptionally friendly.

In this rugged desert, you can understand why in this area man turned to God, how he perceived his dependency on other people, on nature and on the Creator. I could see why Moses led the Jews to Israel, rather than in pursuit of oil in southern Arabia. Here there are riches greater than those that man assesses as riches. Men lived here in caves, and built unusual catacombs for their departed ones. One could argue that the stone monuments of the old civilizations did not protect them, but neither will the gas chambers nor the plastic of the twentieth century protect the present civilization. Here, Romans who extorted taxes are no more, similar to the USSR, which is no more. Well, I'm glad there are waves, historical waves, from which everything flows. And I'm glad that there is a historical justice, that dictators find their end. Otherwise, man would really compete with God, as he sometimes tries to. Even rocks considered eternal will eventually disappear.

Like the great Rabbi Akiva, I look at the world through the prism of justice. The sentence of Rabbi Akiva comes to mind: "*Hakol tsafuy v'harshut n'tuna*," "Everything is foreseen, yet the freedom of choice is given." Ideas persist in spite of the laws of nature and in spite of predestination. Man has the obligation and the responsibility to find the right way and to live according to certain moral codes. The idea and method of our behavior may perhaps be as important, or sometimes more important, than what we create. Morality is how we treat our fellow man, assuring his co-existence. I'm glad to be here to be able to say to the Romans and to my contemporary dictators, "I told you so!"

What Romans left behind them are relics and museums, the history of their evil. What old Israel left are lofty ideas of justice and love, and the relationship to God, the Creator. *Tempora mutantur*, times change, like the donkeys on the mountain road. In God's laboratory, you can check layers of generations from Cain and Abel to Hitler and look at inter-human relations, and have a better understanding of what morality is.

Here, one can understand, but not justify the nature of man. However, one cannot understand the crematoria of the twentieth century. This should never have happened in any civilization. This was man's revolt against nature, God, and human values. Morality is not only a prescribed code of inter-human relations, but also the resulting synthesis of their applications.

A visitor from France approached me, and told me that she is agnostic. She asked me whether I believed in God, and I told her, "I believe in nothing else but in the Creator." Then, she started to agree with me. She corrected herself and said that she also believes in God without having a religion. Many visitors here admire the past and don't see the applications for the present. There were many women who were passing me on the road, but none of them had the grace or gentleness of Marie.

Bedouins are very friendly. One was sitting next to me and played an ancient primitive instrument, called a rababa. Another one told me the stories of their life, how they live in caves, and told me some of their jokes. He looked much more serious than his young age which was just in his early twenties.

I think about this place where people were buried and created an eternal grave. I am still trying to forget Marie's body, but her spirit is constantly with me, and I still feel her sweetness so very much, and the last kiss that I gave her in the coffin. Now her face looks at me from the horizon, from the border of heaven and earth. And I tell her, "I love you, baby, with a bond that will never be cut, since I am united with you forever. You are in me till my body will rest next to yours. I'll never forget you, even if my body and interest wanders away from yours. Good night, sweet Marie."

The next morning we left this place, and we went to Mt. Nebo, where Moses is buried. Well, I felt very fortunate, as a man who was supposed to be gassed fifty-six years ago, to achieve this in my life. I was a witness to the death of my mother and father, and other members of my immediate family were gassed while I was jumping out of the train to Auschwitz. This was not caused by natural calamities but by the most cultural people, the Germans. Is there a similarity between their civilization and that of the Romans, whose cruelty did not protect them from disappearance from the world arena..

The history of this desert tells about the permanency of human values. The magnificent full moon was emerging from behind the mountains. I was jealous after hearing about the life of the poor Bedouins, who express their happiness with life and the warmth of their families. My visit to Petra and to the land of the Bible gave me a better understanding and feeling of the transition of life, as we understand it, as only a short segment of the general existence. But witnessing this transition of ages and civilizations eases the pain I experience after the loss of Marie. *Panta rei*, all is flowing and changing.

We passed the Shawbak Castle and the Karak Castle. Here, the Romans and Crusaders caused a lot of problems to the living and brought death to many. But nothing could compare with the Holocaust.

Looking at the desert, I have a better understanding of why it took the Israelites forty years to cross it, and why they rebelled during the period when they had no water. I appreciate the genius of Moses, who was able to liberate those slaves and bring them here, to the entrance of the Promised Land. I looked at the flat fields after we had left the mountains and their gorges, which look like a number of large canyons, all spread out along the road. What a landscape that was! Finally, we got to Madaba, a rather large town whose population had once been one hundred percent Christian. But times had changed and there were only two-percent Christians living here. We stopped in St. George's Orthodox Church from the sixth century with the mosaic of Jerusalem in the middle of the floor. Afterwards, we came to the King Hussein Bridge, and on the way, we stopped to climb Mt. Nebo. This was the most spiritual moment of the trip, when I stepped on the mountain where the greatest human being is supposed to be buried. Here he stood, symbolizing the past, like Marie, and looking into the future, which never came. And I said Kaddish, the prayer for the departed, for him, for Marie, and for the rest of my family.

Finally, we came to Jerusalem, not the city with her present buildings, not with her people, but to Jerusalem as the symbol of sublime justice and holiness, the symbol of ideas, which bring men closer to God. Here, I can feel the building of a nation, more so than I can recognize it by reading and studying. From Moses to Herzl is a historical bridge of an important synthesis of values. Not the graves and monuments of those people, but their spirits, the inheritance of their ideas, are important.

At the grave of David, I think about the great King who presents the political foundation of the Jewish State, whose descendant is supposed to be the Messiah. I am asking, "What should I consider more important: his power, the foundation of the Jewish State, or his private morality?" For me, his morality is the most important.

I stopped with my son, Richard, at the post office, and there in front of us stood a monk and another gentleman. The monk had just left, and I joked with Richard: "If the monk knew who I was, he would kiss my fingers." The young man overheard this and said that he himself is an evangelist, but who am I? Am I a man of the cloth? And Richard answered that I am more important, but he could not reveal it. Well, we had fun.

We went to do the Church of The Holy Sepulchre. And here, we waited for a long time until we passed the grave of Jesus, the grave of a Jew who started it all. From Jesus to Auschwitz, there are only about two thousand years, a wave that is so filled with blood and the life of Jewish masses. Jesus was a wonderful Jew, and in his name, Jews were killed. I wonder how many former Nazis come here and stand in line in front of the coffin of a Jew, one of those whose brothers they tortured. I pass the sepulcher, thinking whether the suffering of Marie, Jesus and millions of other Jews makes any philosophical sense, or if it occurred only as an opposing idea of evil.

The waves of holiness and morality fight against immorality and criminality—Moses, David, Jesus, Herzl—are only small stops in the waves. Different civilizations—Nabataean, Israeli, Roman, Byzantine, Arabs, Turks, Englishmen, Arabs again, Israel—the waves flow and swallow individuals, swallow us.

I walk along the Via Dolorosa, passing the place where Jesus was imprisoned and read the inscription, "*Locus in quo apprehendit Pilatus Jesum et flagellavit*," the place where Pilate apprehended Jesus and beat him. The Ecce Homo arch makes me think about the size of an arch for six million brothers of Jesus, killed by those who believed in Him. I do remember how the Germans almost killed me before they pushed me inside the car to Auschwitz, along with their beatings and the biting of their dogs. I see a similarity of scenes: of the scene of Jesus and of my own, before the Nazis brought the rest of the transport to the gas chambers.

We left the Via Dolorosa through the Damascus Gate, back to a more peaceful atmosphere, away from the noise of merchants, of the children, of visitors, back to the new city of Jerusalem. A number of wheelchair patients came with the gathering of visitors this time. I had never seen so many wheelchair patients here on my previous trips.

Even though Marie's body is not around, her smile and goodness and intelligence stay with me. The loss of her body and closeness of her spirit squeezes my windpipe and pushes my tear glands to produce tears.

The newly opened Cardo Walk attracts people and here, you can buy mementos and pieces of art. This street is not as crowded as the walks in the old city.

We visited the places known from previous trips: the Hadassah Hospital, the university, Yad Vashem, the Western Wall and we went north to Haifa.

What a beautiful view. What a picturesque bay, when you look down from the Bahai Hill to the golden cupola of the Bahai Temple and the shimmering waters of the Mediterranean. We see behind us, the Dan Hotel, and in front, the delights of the setting sun. In the bay we see the navy's installations, the red boats and the shimmering waves. The shore on the right side reaches to the Lebanese border and to the left it stretches the breadth of the Mediterranean Sea.

I do not detect that the spirit of the people is as enthusiastic as forty years ago. There is missing the old idealism, the enthusiasm of the early Zionists and the happiness that they projected by living in the holy land. They are almost embarrassed of Jewishness and they think in global terms. Jewish archaeologists are publishing work indicating a lack of support of an ancient presence of the Jewish State in the areas that are being claimed. I see more and more that this is not the country of my and Marie's dreams. It has become a secular state and a state where the love, which we and others had several decades ago, is not visible.

We went to Zippori, the place where Yehudah Hanasi compiled the Mishna. This is a beautiful location, and we discover that twenty to forty thousand people lived in this place. Since the city did not defend itself, it did not suffer from the Roman invasion as much as the rest of the country.

I finally found peace in Tiberias, on the Sea of Galilee. Richard joked with me, asking me to walk on the calm water. I told him that I would not compete with somebody who did this once before. The nature is peaceful. The only thing that I am missing here for happiness is the gentleness of Marie.

Across the walk from the hotel, the roof cuts into the lake with the white triangle reflecting the afternoon sun. The opposite shore is a pale transition of the lake's surface into the sky. The swallows are flying overhead and the steps of a cat are the only immediate signs of life. This is a twilight zone between an absolute tranquility and an eternal and delicate form of life. Jesus could not have picked a better place to teach. Here, the past is diffused in the present, land in the water, earth, and sky, and life and lifeless existence. I see Marie's face looking at me from behind the horizon.

Again, the sun sets, and the surface of the lake gets an icy, crystal appearance, as if it were the cover of an eternal sarcophagus. I consider, as a last question in my mind, how the transition is desired, violent as the one of my family, of the six million, or prolonged and painful like Marie's. Blowing in the wind are these questions, spiced with tears.

The morning light, the lake, and the sky have almost the same appearance. And they look like the top and the bottom of an open box. Here are the steps of the Apostles. Here, Jesus taught Judaism, but his studies were carried away and wrongly interpreted. Clouds part in places, revealing the pale blue sky, and Marie's face tries to peek through. The imperceptible ways of water flow with the waves of time, and there is timeless music in nature and in me, a unity.

As mentioned before, we went to the grave of the Great Rabbi Akiva, who coined the already quoted saying, "*Hakol tsafuy v'harshut n'tuna*," in spite of predestination and nature's forces, we have the freedom and the obligation to live morally. He perished at the hands of the Romans with his twenty-four thousand pupils, the same number as the number of Jewish residents in my hometown. We might not finish the job, we might even not see any fruits of our efforts, but we must live according to our belief and try our best. As insignificant as I am, as little as I can influence others, my step in the right direction of morality is an important contribution.

Not far from him is the grave of Rambam. Rambam was the superb theoretician, while Akiva was both the theoretician and the practitioner of Judaism. Not far away are the graves of Rabbi Meir Baal Hanes, of Yohanan Ben Zakai and of the other great teachers who extended their arms to God, asking His help in bettering the person and elevating human morality. I came here in the past with my best friend, Marie.

It is a beautiful day when we leave Israel. There is a blue sky and a green sea. We leave the silver trim of the horizon near the shore, and the Carmel Mountains. Goodbye Israel! We are leaving back to the place where I lived most of my life with Marie, where we loved each other, and where she left me alone. Goodbye. I miss you.

* * * * * * *

At the end of the twentieth century, during which our lives were intertwined, a friend sent me a note, in which he wrote: Everything has a beginning, a middle and an ending. Beginnings and endings have more potential for positive feelings than middles do. Endings can be most satisfying when one fulfilled one's hopes. Beginnings are a challenge that hold promise for a better tomorrow, like a seed that may develop into something worthwhile, if we persevere and nurture it well enough.

The forthcoming new millennium is that kind of beginning, a seed awaiting its yield and a new chapter waiting to be written. We shall be more fortunate than our predecessors, because we shall be growing older in the new millennium, thereby benefiting from all the new technologies.

It is an understatement to say that in your lifetime you have survived and transcended the unfathomable. You have climbed the highest mountains. May the forthcoming new millennium find and keep you in good health, surrounded by stimulating books, friends and activities, commensurate with all the suffering you have endured and the sacrifices you have made at the hands of others.

Oh, my dear friend! I thank you for the words flowing from the heart. If you only knew how much more important I consider the bettering of the human spirit and morality than the explosion of technology, and how impossible it is to replace a person that you loved, who is gone forever.

Her last shriek, like nothing I had ever heard before, expressed physical pain from tearing her heart apart. I felt this also, like a somatic pain, as if caused by our united, spiritual being torn apart. But this spirit will never leave me. It will engulf me with its love of justice and of life, which she so much adored, while I move through the last stretch of our common harmonious wave. I feel a gratitude in my heart for all that Marie gave me, for the echo of the Holocaust that we survived together, for the legacy of love and justice to our family and friends and for the affirmation of life.

My grandchild, I told you in the introduction that in order to understand the road to God, you should ask the transparent drop of rain remaining after the storm. Now, after you have found out about the irrational crimes and about the life story of your grandmother, I advise you to also ask the drops of her tears and the tears of others who are around us. Follow these drops when they join the shimmering waves, reflecting the blue skies and sing Hosanna. While you navigate your boat on the crest, look down the valleys and stretch your heart and hand to those who are hopeless and are near drowning.

I also told you a bit about my eternal love for your grandmother and what a great loss her departure was for me.

My last admonition to you, while you build your abstract structure of ideas, is to love God, Whom you are seeking and Whom you don't know, and members of your species, whom you know, with all your heart and with all your might. While you learn the recorded history of the past, study human morality. In your wanderings, you will come to Mt. Sinai and to the Ten Commandments, a reaction to the previous and coexisting immorality. Since we stood at the foot of Mt. Sinai, things have changed for the worse. Your grandmother and I emerged from the greatest violence ever perpetrated in human history. Learn to appreciate freedom, do not take it for granted and do not shirk your responsibility. Otherwise, it might get lost to tyranny.

Love,

Your Grandfather

www.ingramcontent.com/pod-product-compliance
Lightning Source LLC
LaVergne TN
LVHW041615070426
835507LV00008B/261